Adopting Ainsley

Copyright © 2011 Eric C Anderson
All rights reserved.

ISBN: 0-5780-9109-7
ISBN-13: 9780578091099

Adopting Ainsley

There's No Place for a Car Seat on a Motorcycle

Eric C Anderson

Dedication

For Ainsley, you are our sunshine

Contents

Preface — xi

Chapter I: How It All Began — 1

Chapter II: From Here to L.A. and Back Again — 15

Chapter III: Home Sweet Home — 27

Chapter IV: Tucson or Bust — 39

Chapter V: Miraculous Virgin Conception — 51

Chapter VI: Disappointment in the Making — 63

Chapter VII: Disappointment Realized — 73

Chapter VIII: Back to the Paperwork — 81

Chapter IX: Back to L.A. — 89

Chapter X: Meeting the Birth-Mom to Be — 99

Chapter XI: Travels to Las Vegas — 113

Chapter XII: A Little Rain Must Fall — 127

Chapter XIII: If at First You Don't Succeed — 139

Chapter XIV: Close Encounters with the
 Corporate Greed Mongers 149

Chapter XV: From Corporate Greed to Shady
 Characters 159

Chapter XVI: If at First (or Second) You Don't Succeed…173

Chapter XVII: The Best Laid Plans 183

Epilogue 199

Acknowledgements

Family stories are seldom crafted as a solitary affair. Usually there is a cast of characters—openly recognized or not—who help shape the tale that is about to unfold. Such is the case on the pages that follow…but here we know who is about to appear. First, and foremost, I must give a nod to Melanie, my wife and soul partner. She encouraged me to take on this project, to recreate the events from a rapidly fading memory. She is to be pardoned for any errors that follow and to take credit for prose that makes sense. I just pound on key boards; Melanie keeps the orchestra playing on time and in tune. I also need to thank Melanie's parents—Len and Barbara—who put up with my scrambling for writing time, come children or vacation, and for their accepting Ainsley as a member of the family from day one. My parents—Jim and Audrey—deserve an equal accord. I grew up in a house that welcomed and encouraged diversity, we should all be so lucky. Finally, I want to thank Ainsley…she brings a new smile every day of the week. While it is tempting to agree children are a blessing and a curse, I'll take the sunshine with the rain at any turn of the page.

Preface

Well enough for old folks to rise early, because they have done so many mean things all their lives they can't sleep anyhow.

—*Mark Twain*

    I have never been a sound sleeper. Despite an irrational tendency to rise before the sun and head for a local gym, I typically find myself up and about two-to-three times a night. My wife, who wisely subscribes to the theory sleeping pills were invented for a reason, has tolerated this behavior for years. Occasionally she'll convince me to choke down one of her sleep aids, but the result is less than satisfying and I don't enjoy the morning after stupor—particularly when I'm engaged in hoisting dumbbells over my relatively fragile noggin. So I do without, choosing instead to rely on coffee and catnaps at my desk. And then we adopted Ainsley.

    After three months of cringing at whimpers and moans emitting from the front bedroom—also known as the cave of the beast—I am thoroughly convinced alarm clock manufacturers need to revisit the drawing board. Bells, chimes, and loud music be damned…there is nothing that will wake a sleeper faster than a baby's wail. And there is nothing more likely to keep one from hitting the drowse button than the odor associated with a fully laden diaper. In short, I have gone from being a fitful sleeper to a cowering napper. My subconscious is perpetually on alert for the first signal all is not well in Ainsley's world.

    It's only fair to state Melanie, my wife, also suffers this malady. I can now safely state that even drugs intended to subdue elephants are insufficient for drowning out the cries of a three-month old child. So down the hallway she'll go, staggering in her drug-induced haze. Frankly, I'm impressed. In the old days—before we adopted Ainsley—Melanie could sleep though my alarm clock, exhibiting few signs of life as I prepared for yet another round in the weight room. I thought that would still be the case after Ainsley came home. I was wrong. Melanie too has succumbed to the fear that, unattended, the whimpering will quickly escalate into a full-volume howl. Better to put out the flames before they become a raging blaze.

My own thoughts? I am now afraid of nights. More than once Melanie has caught me perusing military assignment options in Afghanistan or Iraq. I'd rather take on the Taliban or contend with insurgents than quiver under the sheets waiting for the next demand for a midnight feeding or diapering services. At least in Afghanistan and Iraq I would be allowed to fire back at the enemy. With Ainsley I am compelled to coo and gurgle—an unsightly and slightly demeaning act for any male—but particularly for one who is in his mid-forties, tattooed, and pretty sure he can still think or fight his way out of most unpleasant predicaments.

And if all this is not bad enough, let me tell you what happens once the sun does come up. While Ainsley blissfully snoozes the day away, her parents are engaged in endless conversations concerning sleep duration, milk consumption, and the color of the latest diaper load. That's right. We actually spend hours comparing notes on these developments with other functional, productive adults.

We are not alone. As a lot, new parents delight in sharing the fact they "finally" got four hours of sleep last night, or that a particular formula mix seems to minimize baby flatulence. (Trust me; babies issue more gas than a 40-man tent after a heady meal of rice and beans.) Whatever happened to discussions concerning politics or world affairs? Babies, it seems, are a none-too subtle means of reducing even the Washington crowd to the lowest common denominator. My insights on China won't hold a dinner table for more than five minutes…my latest story about accidentally sticking my finger into an odiferous diaper, on the other hand, will rivet the guests' attention for hours.

You know who gets the biggest kick out of this situation? Our parents. While she will never admit it, I'm willing to bet that Melanie's parents threatened her with the same curse my folks used to invoke. "Some day you'll have a child just like you." Well maybe it's a little early in Ainsley's life to pull out that old favorite. After all, at three-months she has yet to break the china, pull the dog's tail, or run away from home. Furthermore, she cannot yet hold her breath and threaten to turn blue, or wrap Dad around her finger through sweet talk and batted eyes. Nope, all Ainsley can resort to is tears…and to be quite fair, she doesn't even do that with undue frequency.

So while our parents can exchange knowing looks—and then head for home—and our friends have resigned themselves to weekly emails of cute baby pics and endless discussions about our sleepless nights, Melanie and I have begun the life-long adaptation process. That is, we are learning to become Mom and Dad. The way I see it, billions of other people have survived this grueling training, we should be able to at least hold our own in the crowd. Who knows? We might even be good at it…but first we need to survive the witching hours…that dread time period between 10pm and 4:30am, where we pretend to sleep…and Ainsley conjures up new means of summoning the dead.

But life with a wee infant is not why I'm parked in front of the computer. Nor is it the reason you're reading this book. I'm here to tell the story about how Ainsley came into our lives. How two middle-aged professionals managed to adopt a child without leaving our shores. You see, Ainsley is not from China, Ethiopia or Russia. She is a domestic product, manufactured right here in the

United States. Finding her was no easy feat. In the pages that follow I hope to provide a feel for the travel, travails, and twerps one encounters upon entering the world of private adoption.

    This is not a tale for the faint of heart, the politically correct, or misers. Suffice it to say we had our ups, downs, and wrote a lot of checks. And, despite my continuing need for a nap, it was worth every expended minute and dollar.

Chapter I
How it All Began

The proverb says that Providence protects children and idiots. This is really true. I know because I have tested it.

—Mark Twain

Allow me to open with confessions. As a part-time educator and a full-time national security consultant, I've learned its best to divulge the ugly facts first. Why? Well revelation of potentially embarrassing information has a way of grabbing the audience's attention. Students like to know I can't spell and have never learned to pronounce half the words I pretend to keep in my vocabulary. (Try to spit out "fortuitously" in front of a room full of bright-eyed college students. I never get it right—that's why Webster includes "happily" in the dictionary.) My government clients want to know if the North Koreans are planning to come over the border tomorrow, then they ask questions about my arcane ideas for keeping Pyongyang in the box. And, I suspect you would like to know something about us before I explain why we engaged in an 18-month hunt for our new daughter.

So here goes. As unvarnished as possible. I am a white male, in his mid-40s (my friends, annoyingly, keep telling me to change that adjective to "late"), who suffers a significant case of adult attention deficiency. Which is a fancy way of saying I can't seem to settle on a career. Having walked out of academia in the early 1990s, I have managed to tour the world as an Air Force intelligence officer, hang out in Hawaii as a civilian analyst, and now find myself banished to Washington DC. Along the way I've acquired a few tattoos, put over 200,000 miles on a variety of motorcycles, and managed to screw up two marriages. (Subtle advice for the female reader, stay away from men who prefer two-wheeled transportation, older whiskey, and the accumulation of frequent-flyer miles.) I also have a son who is turning 10—and can readily defeat his father's attempts at logic in two languages.

I showed up in Washington in 2005—an eligible bachelor with no real interest in pursuing more than a good Harley repair shop and a cold beer. Having managed to live on my sailboat in Hawaii for almost three years and then disappear to Iraq for 6 months, I was as unencumbered as a man could be. That is to say, I owned no furniture, had given away my books, and spent my evenings turning wrench on a pair of very dirty motorcycles. Why wash them when you can ride?

I know, I know, some readers are going to think I was living the life of Riley. No lawn to mow, no dog to walk, and no one to tell me what to wear or eat. Trust me; ribeye with merlot is a good meal…five or six times a week. Happy hour hors d'oeuvres are always a handy option when one doesn't want to cook. There was just one problem—I was lonely. Back to the confessions. I am a people-person. Unlike many of my counterparts in the intelligence community, I actually enjoy mingling with other humans. Furthermore, I actually don't complain about having Melanie pick my clothes or set our social agenda. I have no talent for either.

In any case, after a year of hanging out in the nation's capitol I was finally convinced that my dating life needed a radical overhaul. The bar scene was not for me and blind dates were not a promising option. Too many unpleasant surprises. The solution, according to one of my counterparts at work, was to go on-line. He urged me to sell my soul on Match.com. Needless to say, I was skeptical. There seemed little to be gained from placing my picture and answers to arcane questions—what is your favorite astrological sign?—and much to lose. For one thing, such personal ads have a nasty tendency to suddenly show up on the bulletin board at work. If mortification is not deterrent enough, there is always the fear of who might actually respond to that ad…still sends shudders down my spine.

Now I don't want to brag, but my ad was online for only about a week when Melanie found me. This is not to say I managed to avoid all the potential pitfalls associated with such a posting. There were at least three marriage proposals from Russian would-be brides fishing for a sucker—or a green card. But on the whole, I found the experience relatively painless and tremendously rewarding. Eight months later I was married to the woman of my dreams…and the dedicated walker of a delightful dog and caretaker for a 150-year old townhouse. The dog we kept, the house now has new owners.

Enough about me, lets meet Melanie. Melanie is 5 foot 3 inch petite dynamo. Three years younger than I, she has academic and professional credentials that put my track record to shame. A lawyer who once worked as an Assistant United States Attorney, Melanie now runs a non-profit that specializes in unmasking unethical politicians and their nefarious plots. To say Melanie is opinionated is an understatement. More appropriate terms would be deeply committed and driven. She is also, as you might suspect, never wanting for work. Furthermore, after years of dating and fishing around on Match.com, Melanie was sick of kissing frogs…and was interested in starting a family.

Now here's the problem with "old" people getting married. While your average 20-year old can seemingly reproduce at will, we seasoned types have to actually work at accomplishing this feat. (Those of you who are easily embarrassed should skip ahead a few paragraphs…what follows might make you blush.) What we figured this meant was a little more time engaged in bedroom gymnastics. A not unpleasant thought—at least for this red-blooded American male—but one that rapidly became a chore.

Eric C Anderson

That's right, sex can become work. This is particularly true if you are looking at a calendar and are rapidly coming to the realization that time waits for no man or woman. Do the math with me. If we succeed at this procreation process, a big if, the bun then has to sit in the oven for 9 months. That would find each of us another year older—to say nothing of discomfort associated with pregnancy. Nonetheless, we were willing to try. So let the games begin.

Lacking medical degrees, but absent no end of recommendations from friends and acquaintances, we chose to increase our odds by doing some on-line education. This is how the thermometer came to live on Melanie's nightstand. Seems there is a theory that changes in a woman's temperature reflect progress in the 30-day ovulation cycle. Catch the days when the temperature is up and one's odds of getting pregnant are supposed to increase. Here's the catch, you have to take that measurement at the same time every day…preferably in the early morning. So each morning at 5:45 I would turn off the alarm and Melanie would reach for the digital thermometer. While she sat and waited for the machine to do its magic, I would doze. The sound of the thermometer beeping indicated the job was done and it was time for me to climb out of bed.

All well and good, except now our sex life went from a relatively spontaneous event—hey, I like to be surprised with a silk negligee as much as the next guy—to a forced march. Come home from work at 7, drop my lunch box in the kitchen and then head for the bedroom. Not much romance in this, but at least we could claim to be putting in the old college try. And so we did, for over five months. All to no avail. Along the way we got to experiment with a large number of pregnancy test kits and try a few new positions, but no baby. Frustrating.

Of course, the whole time we're engaged in this process the lingering fear of birth defects and/or mental retardation was a nagging concern. Old people have a hard time reproducing for a reason. While only about 9% of total pregnancies occur in women 35 years or older each year, about 25% of babies with Down syndrome are born to women in this age group. A frightening statistic. Melanie and I had agreed at the outset we were not prepared to raise a child with these disabilities, so this made the whole get pregnant at home trick just that much harder.

Oh, while I am on the subject, when did pregnancy become a "we" thing? I was a little astonished the first time I encountered the phrase "we are pregnant." Don't get me wrong, I'm all about sharing the load, but there is little "we" in pregnancy. I get to participate in the fun part, and then step back and offer sympathy as Melanie waddles around for nine uncomfortable months. That, and I get to pass on the whole delivery process. Sure, I'll stand in the room and observe the medical team at work, but there is no football passing between my legs at the end the day. In short, "we" don't get pregnant, but enough of my tirade, back to the story at hand.

At the same time we were working on reproductive drills at home, Melanie initiated a search for an adoption agency. This is not as easy as one might think. Go on the internet and type "adoption." Google returns with over 96 million options. Type in "adoption agency" and you get over 2 million choices. "Adoption attorney" about halves that number, as does "adoption lawyer," but you get my point. A decision to pursue adoption immediate opens the door to an overwhelming set of options.

Or so you think at first blush. When we looked at the international options we were suddenly confronted with a limited set of choices. Many nations have limits on age, number of previous marriages, and require candidates be married for anywhere between 12 months and 10 years prior to applying. And then there is the waiting period. The bare minimum is 12 months. Most international programs will tell you to expect a wait of 24-60 months.

Eric C Anderson

Now we're back to that damn calendar. If we sign up for one of the international programs the child we were seeking could arrive in time for my 50th birthday. I'm a brave man, but not stupid. I have friends who adopted at 50. They turned 60 overnight.

Nonetheless, we made an appointment with an agency that specialized in Ethiopian adoptions. Why Ethiopia? Well, the criteria were favorable for our circumstances, the wait was only 12 months, and known risks were largely limited to malnutrition. The same cannot be said for the Russian children. Warehoused in what might best be described as holding pens, the Russian kids come with a high risk of fetal alcohol syndrome and attachment disorder. The first malady stunts intellectual development, the second significantly increases your chances of living with a mentally disturbed child. So we struck Russia from the list.

Here's the drawback to Ethiopia. Melanie has a strong dislike of flying and a firm belief that hotels are best evaluated by sheet thread count—400 or higher—the provision of cotton balls, and accessibility to outstanding restaurants. "Fine dining" will not suffice, it has to be outstanding. We once spent a long weekend in Paris. While I prepared by expending three hours reading guidebooks and selecting known tourist traps, Melanie consumed three weeks sorting through restaurant guides and recommendations. There were no accidental meals during the sojourn. The same thing, by the way, is true when we eat out in Washington or anywhere else in the country. So one can imagine her dismay upon being informed we would be spending 10 days in Ethiopia. All that said, we were still seriously looking into the possibility.

As for options closer to home, well let me tell you a story. Both Melanie and I have gone through the District of Columbia foster care program. We both walked away in complete frustration. A year before we met, Melanie went through the entire program and then was informed she would be a poor choice because her expectations of a child would be "too high." Even more disturbingly, she was discouraged from continuing with the process because she wasn't African-American.

When I attended the foster care program initiation I was informed the process would require attendance of a seemingly endless series of classes, and then there was little possibility of being offered a chance to adopt anyone younger than 12. Melanie and I frequently do not see eye-to-eye on politics or my motorcycle addiction, but we firmly agreed the commitment of time we were prepared to make should benefit someone not already set in his or her ways. In short, we wanted to take the chance at screwing up our own kid, not having someone else do this for us.

I will admit the District of Columbia foster program is intended to meet a crying need, but it also provided a few of my lighter moments in dealing with bureaucrats. The initial meeting for the foster program is slated for 9 am on Saturday mornings. Seeking to be perceived as a responsible adult, I showed up 10 minutes early. At 9:00, the program facilitator walked in the room and promptly announced the nine o'clock show time was intended to ensure we were all present by 9:30 and the event would only begin at that point. I read the *Wall Street Journal* twice that morning.

The second bit of levity came halfway through the 9:30 presentation. After explaining how the process worked, and the compensation associated with taking on a foster child, we were invited to ask questions. Hands shot up throughout the room. As one might expect, most of these questions involved clarification of information provided in the initial presentation. However, one gentleman clearly had other thoughts on his mind. His question, "After getting paid, do we have to love these children?" At which point the woman next to him hauled off with a heavy hand to the back of his head. I'll never know if it was his wife or just an outraged citizen, but I do know the incident left the room in stitches.

Eric C Anderson

I'm off on a tangent again, back to Ethiopia. In early March 2008 we had a meeting with a representative from a highly recommended adoption agency that maintained extensive contacts in the destitute country. Clearly the bedroom gymnastics weren't working, so progress on any other front seemed productive. After an hour session the agency rep declared we would be good candidates for their program…but startled us by outlining the associated paperwork odyssey. I have held a top secret clearance for 20 years, and had never done this much paperwork. Apparently my ability to be trusted with issues affecting our national security is less suspect than my ability to adopt and raise a child. Oh, and did I mention you don't have to do any of this if you can simply produce a child at home?

What am I complaining about? Here's the list…and there is more to come. Before you can even think about formally applying to adopt you must provide:

- Personal Information: This includes names, every address where you have resided, birth date, social security numbers, employers, salaries, phone numbers, and email addresses.
- General Information: Who resides in your home, including the name, age, and gender of each person. You will also have to report on the relation of each person to the family in the home. Melanie kept including the dog, I'm just glad they did not ask for a pecking order in this list…the dog always comes before me, a dark family secret that scientists have proven applies in most households.
- Adoption Information: This includes an essay on why you want to adopt—the reasons and motivations. I refer to this as the "why I want to attend your college" section of the paperwork.
- Medical Information: On the adoptive parents and anyone else residing in the house. This includes any medical conditions and/or history. They literally mean "warts and all."

- Financial Information: You will get to disclose the contents of your checking and savings account, as well as any other financial accounts. The claim is that this to ensure you can afford to care for the child, I'm very suspicious that the agencies are simply checking to ensure you can pay their extravagant bills.
- Criminal Background Check: Criminal background checks may be conducted for every county you have lived in for the last 15 number of years—no problem for Melanie, bad karma for me…I've lost track of the places the military has sent me.
- Birth Certificates: Copies of birth certificates for each parent—after the criminal background check you would think this was redundant—never try to out think a bureaucrat.
- Marriage Certificate: Please observe they must be notarized copies of your marriage certificate, no photocopies are permitted.
- Fingerprints: Yup, a free trip to the local police department…only to be told they don't do this for would-be adoptive parents—that requires a trip to a private firm and $50.
- References: Typically three letters from non-family members. I have to admit this was a relief, I'm not sure my Mother's comments on my childhood would have resulted in anyone allowing me near another small person.

I'm exhausted just thinking about it now. Over the course of about three weeks this is all we did at night. Answer questions and root about for obscure data. And, as it turned out, the local criminal background check was only the beginning. In the end we had an opportunity to send our fingerprints off to the Federal Bureau of Investigations for their official blessing. If you have anything you want to hide from your spouse, adoption is out. By the time we finished all these forms Melanie no longer had to ask questions about my past—it was all there in front of her in black and white… and triplicate.

Meanwhile, having still not succeeded in conceiving at home, we also began to explore the option of private adoption. Before I turn to that conversation, we have a loose end on the reproductive front that needs to be addressed. Given our failure in the bedroom, why not go with *In vitro* fertilization? *In vitro* fertilization is a procedure that allows egg cells to be fertilized by sperm outside the womb. The long and short of this process—the sperm get to have all their fun in a pitre dish…you don't even get to watch.

Here's the problem, *in vitro* is expensive—about $10,000 a pop—and does not remove the risk for birth defects I mentioned earlier. Furthermore, there is a possibility the fertilized egg will not take in the womb, resulting in a failed pregnancy. Oh, I forgot the "best" part. The associated fertility drugs frequently cause significant mood swings. Melanie is moody enough already…we weren't sure we would still be married after a couple of months in this cycle. For all these reasons we decided to opt out. It was now adoption or nothing.

Private adoption is the route of choice for Americans who either are not qualified for the international option or choose to avoid the wait and paperwork hassles. Oh, it is also only an option if you can afford the bills. This ain't cheap. Private domestic adoption generally refers to process by which U.S.-born infants are directly placed with the "adopting parents." (Not to be confused with the "birth parents"…you know, the people who actually had the baby.) Private adoptions can be accomplished in a number of manners, including the assistance of facilitators, doctors, clergy, or attorneys. But don't count on using the first three—this is a niche career attorneys have almost completely cornered.

Private domestic adoption is also a dying industry. As we discovered, increased access to contraception, the legalization of abortion, and widespread social acceptance of unmarried parenting, have caused the number of infants placed for adoption in the U.S. to decline dramatically. According to the Evan B. Donaldson Adoption Institute, "between 1989 and 1995, 1.7% of children born to never-married white women were placed for adoption, compared to 19.3% before 1973. Among never-married black women, relinquishment rates have ranged from 0.2% to 1.5%."

At the same time, the birth rate among women of peak childbearing age has also been declining. Birth rates for women in their 20s and early 30s are generally down while births to older mothers (35-44) are still on the rise. As Melanie will tell you, this can be explained by factors other than access to contraceptives and legalized abortion. This decline in birth rates for younger women reflects the fact females in American society have entered the workplace and like being competitive. It's damn hard to maintain a career and care for a toddler—particularly when younger employees are expected to demonstrate their commitment by working longer hours.

In short, we were investigating an option that was a seller's, not a buyer's, market. This was particularly true if we were interested in a white child. Time for a little more personal disclosure. I have little interest in a person's religion, ethnicity, nationality or skin color. My first wife was Buddhist, the second Catholic, and Melanie is Jewish. My son is half Korean. My brother's wife is Muslim and was born in Calcutta, India. (All this once prompted my mother—a fair-haired Scandinavian—to remark, "What's the matter with blondes?" I think it was my brother who replied, "Boring." Her tossed shoe missed his head by inches.) In any event, I really had no interest in pursuing the blonde, blue-eyed baby. I like diversity—even if it results in a lot of curious glances and questions.

Melanie is equally unbiased. Raised in Wilmington, Delaware—home of preppy styles like embroidered belts for men and bold print flower dresses for women—she was exposed to a WASP-dominated environment that was not always open-minded about issues like faith or race. As a result, Melanie grew up a bit of an outsider. I suspect the education she received at a Quaker Friends

School helped ease the associated pain, and left her very attuned to society's capricious biases. The consequence of our perspectives, a circle of friends and acquaintances that is all-encompassing. (Actually, I knew Melanie was open-minded from the outset…she did agree to marry me.) What this really meant in the long-run was that the fair-skinned child who looked like us was at the bottom of our list of priorities.

This approach to creating a family, by the way, is relatively uncommon. In our conversation with various adoption attorneys it quickly became apparent that waiting times dropped significantly—literally in half—if we were interested in a child of mixed or other racial composition.

Having thus resolved the racial issue, we set about the process of finding a private adoption service. This is trickier than you might think. It turns out the law in some states allows attorneys and other individuals who are not licensed as child-placing agencies to match adoptive parents with birth parents. In most states, however, the adoptive and birth parents must make initial contact with one another absent the intervention of an individual, such as an attorney, who is receiving professional fees for rendering services in connection with the adoption proceeding. In these states, the adoptive and birth parents must make initial contact with one another by such means as word of mouth and newspaper advertising. This helps explain those "couple seeking child" ads one encounters in local papers and on the internet.

As best we could tell, the most user-friendly states in 2008 were California, Florida and Texas. Hmmm. All of the options potentially involved a lot of flying, as I've noted, not Melanie's favorite event. What to do? We could plan on hanging out with the movie crowd in L.A., the folks who elected George W. Bush to his first public office, or contemplate suffering Miami's heat and another Bush-friendly audience. We went with the movie stars. Well, the decision wasn't quite that flip.

Identifying the person who is going to help change your life forever is best not accomplished using the internet, Yellow Pages or political leanings. Unfortunately, Consumer Reports has yet to publish an annual evaluation of adoption attorneys...so we went with personal suggestions. One of Melanie's acquaintances had just successfully employed the offices of Alfred Book in her quest to adopt and offered a glowing recommendation. We took the bait...hook, line, and sinker. Two phone calls later we were prospective clients. The one hitch? We needed to be in Los Angeles for a day long interview. As I said, a lot of time in airports and on jets...a lot of time.

Chapter II
From Here to L.A. and Back Again

Travel has no longer any charm for me. I have seen all the foreign countries I want to except heaven and hell, and I have only a vague curiosity about one of those.

—*Mark Twain, 20 May 1891*

Our nation's capitol is notable for many reasons, easy connections to the rest of America is not one of them. I have friends who argue this is not accidental. "After all," they like to remind me, "the city is full of people who are clearly out of touch with the rest of the country." There has to be a rational reason for this….something beyond delusions of propriety and inspired proprietorship. Alas, I respond. We can explain the problem. It is not metaphysical, it is the absence of well thought-out airports.

You see, in the DC area we have three options: Reagan National, Dulles, and Baltimore Washington International. Reagan National (referred to as "Reagan" if you are a Republican and "National" if you are a Democrat) is home to a ragtag collection of connecting flights. Allow me to illustrate. We once flew from Reagan National to Paris—via Chicago. On a second occasion we made it to Italy via Raleigh Durham. Reagan National is where one heads if New York is high on your list…everyone else can plan on at least one stop en route your final destination. It also has the slowest baggage handlers in the United States. Reagan National is best employed in emergencies and for business trips, which brings us to the other two options.

Eric C Anderson

Dulles. Dulles International Airport is best considered a classic example of 1950s bureaucratic incompetence. Constructed 26 miles outside the nation's capitol, Dulles has no rail or subway connection, and offers—at best—spotty bus links to Washington proper. (The taxi services, as one might suspect, are not complaining.) The parking has been arranged in a manner intended to increase one's odds of missing a flight, and the security lines are inevitably long. And that's before you try to get from the main terminal to your gate. Apparently intent on sharing the scenic runaway activities with as many passengers as possible, the original Dulles architects decided we would all be best served by employing giant buses that careen about the tarmac. Vaguely space shuttle-like in appearance, these buses are sure to be packed, slow, and inconveniently timed. The only thing that saves Dulles is a large collection of direct flights to almost anywhere on the entire planet.

Finally, a comment on Baltimore Washington International. Located 30 miles north of the capitol, BWI is a quaint facility that claims to be the 24th busiest airport in the United States. Unlike Dulles, BWI is actually served by a rail connection, but most people drive. Here's where the drawback emerges. While Dulles sits at the end of a dedicated expressway, BWI is best reached via the Baltimore-Washington Parkway. This is an aptly named highway, as any accident or inconsiderate driving does indeed turn this bit of pavement into a parking facility. The airlines have caught on to this problem, and seek to compensate by offering lower fares for BWI. Few of us are fooled. Unless you are a glutton for punishment or have all day to waste on a 30 mile trip, BWI is out.

A long-time Washington resident, Melanie is well-aware of this airport handicap. She will spend hours researching the best flight options and seeking a means of avoiding airport terminal food. (With one exception, McDonalds. For reasons beyond my comprehension, Melanie—the resident food snob—likes McDonalds's egg sandwiches for breakfast. I, personally, have sworn off that entire meal, so no big deal for me. But I can tell you we have

Adopting Ainsley

walked great distances in airport terminals searching for a Mickey Ds.) As a result she knows you can get to L.A. non-stop once a day from Reagan National, that Dulles is best employed between 11 o'clock and 3 (avoid rush hour traffic), and that BWI is only considered an emergency backup.

This airport conundrum became an important part of our lives the minute we decided to employ Alfred. Encouraged by our acquaintance's experience, we scheduled a flight to L.A. in May 2008. Melanie managed to get us booked on a direct flight from Reagan National and succeeded in obtaining a rental car that was not located on a lot three miles from LAX. She also discovered we would be spared two nights in L.A. if we agreed to the attorney's request for a 10:30 sit down. All's well, or so it would appear.

Like doctors and dentists, all attorneys do not graduate at the top of their class. The resulting variances in health care providers can be frightening…the difference in attorney skill sets is just damn aggravating. Suffice it to say Alfred, like most lawyers specializing in private adoption, did not finish at the top of his class—or in the top half. (Melanie's observation was even more astute—she suspects he graduated in the bottom half of the bottom schools.) In fact, I'm now suspicious Alfred was the John McCain of his class. That is, he garnered no academic honors and just managed to meet matriculation requirements.

Our first hint this might be the case? Despite multiple emails confirming our 6 hour (yes, 6 hour) intake interview was going to begin at 10:30, we arrived at his offices only to discover Alfred was nowhere to be found. To make matters worse, his staff was not overly concerned about his unexplained absence. "Oh, yes," we were reassured, "he'll be here, we're just not sure when." Melanie, who has no patience for such buffoonery, gave me a look that has been known to wither the stuffiest of French waiters. I shrugged my shoulders—often the best response in such situations—and began interrogating the staff. That, at least, satisfied Melanie, who went off to do email on her Blackberry. I was condemned to sipping bad coffee and listening to the staff randomly attempt to locate their boss.

It's only fair to note I also suffer fools poorly. On more than one occasion I have quietly suggested cranial-anal inversion. Sometimes not so quietly. In this case, I used an unoccupied desktop to surf the web in search of other nearby adoption attorneys. Fastest way to spur staff action, start dialing competitors' offices and loudly discuss options for setting up an appointment…in, oh, say, the next 30 minutes. The search for Alfred suddenly assumed an air of urgency polite requests had been unable to motivate.

Why this demand for punctuality? Suffice it to say Alfred was not doing us a favor. His purported 6-hour intake interview cost $800 dollars and included a session with a local psychologist and a good deal of paperwork—much of which we had previously accomplished. Furthermore, the whole show came with a bit of pretentiousness. Alfred appeared to imply he would determine if we were qualified for his services and to be parents. I, on the other hand, felt we were suffering this waste of time as a means of determining whether or not Alfred should be the recipient of our hard-earned money. Needless to say, the two parties were not on the same wavelength.

Unfortunately for us, Alfred waddled in the door at about 11 o'clock. This was not an inspiring sight. About six feet tall, Alfred is at least 50 pounds overweight, tanned from apparently smoking his cigarettes pool-side, and quite clearly suffering a substance abuse problem. The blood-shot eyes, rumpled clothing, and perpetually flushed face suggested a fondness for drink that only ended when the bottle was empty. And he was going to determine if we were fit to be his clients and potentially mom and dad. My confidence in this process reached new lows.

Adopting Ainsley

Melanie, on the other hand, suddenly became quite cooperative. I will never understand why, but Melanie—who will eat a professional politician's career for lunch—is unwilling to take that same hard approach to dealing with her fellow attorneys. Needless to say, I was dumbfounded by this change in attitude. In less time than it takes to say "Jackie Robinson," Melanie had jabbed me in the ribs, whispered a firm "cooperate" in my ear, and was ready to sit through whatever Alfred was willing to offer. I'm slow, but not stupid; I shook hands with the wayward attorney and shut my mouth.

Alfred used the next hour to fill in gaps...mostly in our understanding of how the billing process worked. He haphazardly asked why we wanted to be parents, and sniffed around our interest in children who were not lily-white. We passed the test on finances and seemed to scratch his cursory itch concerning our commitment to raising a child. Then he asked a zinger. "Boy or girl?"

I come from a family of boys. Something in our genetic code keeps spitting out males. My parents had two, my brother had two, and my sister had two. Sister? You mumble, I thought he said only boys. My sister, it turns out, is also adopted. My parents understood the heavy curse coursing through their veins and opted to find an easier means of determining a child's sex. My sister, on the other hand, appears to have been infected by the bug. Oh, and yes, I have a son.

Little boys can be fun. There is much to be said of boundless energy, a willingness to play most sports, and a desire to kill everything that walks, crawls or flys. These endearing features can also be significant deterrents. I have found myself spending 5 hours in the swimming pool. I have also sat through baseball games wondering at an entire team's inability to catch or hit, and worried when the Tai Kwon Do instructor suggested breaking blocks with one's head. Furthermore, the fascination with death and killing can become overwhelming...particularly if you really liked the gold fish or ever thought every flower in the neighborhood was not in need of beheading.

Not "blessed" with my experiences, Melanie had her own reasons for preferring a daughter. Girls, she would argue, are more fun to shop for, think flowered pink dresses are cute, and will happily sit through yet another episode of "General Hospital." In addition, Melanie believes a girl will like to cook, may be less likely to pull the dog's tail, and could delight in spending hours reading the collected works of Jane Austin. In short, Melanie was looking for a mall soul-mate, not an excuse to hang out at the local pool hall. We told Alfred, we really wanted a daughter.

I was only slightly surprised to learn this is a common desire among older parents. (See, we do get wiser with the passage of time.) Seems we as a society have become less obsessed with perpetuating our family name and more concerned about raising a manageable child. I would also note, however, that many people have warned me about the "ease" associated with managing a teenage daughter. Boys, they lecture, can be cuffed around the ears and understand a little physical intimidation is necessary. Girls will brook no such nonsense; choosing instead to engage in psychological warfare. (My father-in-law made a very similar argument… he should know, he survived two daughters.) So who is right? Don't know, I have another 13 years before learning the answer.

In any case, we unanimously chimed in with "girl," and awaited Alfred's next question. Damn good thing we weren't holding our breath. Instead of proceeding with the interrogation, our erstwhile attorney opted to provide a dire warning about the type of people commonly volunteering to be birth mothers. To use his words, "there are very few Brigham Young freshmen calling in a panic after missing their first period." Instead, we were informed the best we could hope for was minimal drug and alcohol use, some prenatal care, and a request for support both before and after the delivery.

Adopting Ainsley

This support issue is no minor matter. In fact, I am suspicious there are women who use the private adoption process as a means of earning a living for up to six months at time. You see, support in this case can include transportation, rent, medical care, maternity clothes, food, and entertainment. Yup, you can find yourself paying for cable TV. So as to prevent your losing track of all these bills, the adoption attorneys typically handle the expenses by establishing a slush fund…oops, I mean trust fund. A pool of your money they thoughtfully disburse and then bill you for hours expended. As best I could tell this was an ideal situation for the birth mother and the lawyer…they were being paid. We, on the other hand, began considering second jobs.

According to Alfred, we need not fear the expenses. In his version of reality, we would sign a contract with the mother agreeing to set amounts and then he would reasonably handle the resulting obligations. There was little we could do but agree to such an arrangement. But before signing any bottom line I wanted to see a few examples of other people's agreements. Alfred's clear reluctance to comply with this request should have been a warning sign. In truth, we should have walked out after he showed up 30 minutes late—but now we were witnessing his true colors.

After stammering about prices ranging from $25,000 to $40,000, Alfred finally requested his legal assistant pull a few agreements from the files and give us sanitized versions. I suspect he meant the names and personal data were to be redacted. Instead we were handed copies of the signed contracts absent one thing, the final sunk cost. Sure, we now knew many of the mothers were earning between $1,500 and $2,000 a month. We also now understood the support agreements could carry on up to two months after the child was born, but still had no idea what all the medical, legal and sundry expenses might add up to. And Alfred sure as hell was not cooperating by trying to answer that question. The best he would do…totals approaching $38,000…situation dependent.

Eric C Anderson

Can you imagine going into any other business arrangement with this kind of fiscal fuzziness? Hmmm, let me rephrase that. Can you image anyone but the federal government entering into a legal contract involving a clear deliverable without knowing how much you could ultimately expect to spend? Prior to our foray into the world of adoptions I sure couldn't. Interestingly, Alfred acted as though we were the first people to demand such specific cost estimates. As best I could tell, his reaction to our questions implied 99% of his clients didn't care what they spent; they just wanted to emerge as parents.

I would also note Alfred was not unique in assuming this position. The world of adoption is rife with the potential for exploitation. The agencies and attorneys in this field understand they are working with people who desperately want to become parents. They also know said would-be parents tend to be older and wealthier. After all, if their clients were young and poor they would be home making babies…maybe four or five of them. We couldn't do that, and thus were readily susceptible to price gouging. Let me be quite blunt, private adoption in the United States is a profit-oriented business. The only difference between individuals engaged in this line of work and those selling cars; the product is a human being.

Having thus succeeded in raising our blood pressure, Alfred decided this would be a good time to bring in his contract social worker/psychologist. While Alfred was the antithesis of the stereotypical California lifestyle, his side-kick psychologist was embodiment of what every Midwestern believes they will encounter when driving the streets of LA. Adorned in designer jeans, sockless loafers, and a shirt unbuttoned to mid chest, the psychologist sported a ponytail and enough jewelry to be the envy of every 15 year-old girl. Furthermore, he was tanned, tanned, tanned…and could speak fluent valley girl without apparent concentration. The military side of me screamed for a good set of hair clippers and a dress code. Melanie, aware of my internal musing in such situations, refocused my attention with a swift, out-of-sight kick to the shin.

And then the questioning really began. We were once again grilled on how we lived, what we did for fun, and where we believed our lives were heading. (I didn't realize having children required all this psychological musing.) We were asked about our relationships with friends and family. (Friends, no sweat....that's why they're called friends. Family...my bet, no one answers this in an entirely truthful manner.) Finally, 45 minutes into the inquisition, came the real topper. "Tell me about your drug use."

Pause. Melanie looked at me, I looked at her, and the psychologist stared at us both. I've had a top secret clearance for 20 years. I also serve in the Air Force reserve. In either case, I am subject to random urinalysis and potential follow-on screening. I like being able to pay the bills and providing food for the table, so smoking pot, sniffing glue, or snorting coke is out. Melanie, as a former prosecutor and current executive director of an ethics watch dog group is equally under the spotlight. Quite frankly, there is no marijuana growing in our backyard, nor do we partake in the consumption of any other illegal substance.

That response, surprisingly, didn't scratch his itch. "Have you ever used illegal substances?" Who was this clown? I managed to spend the entire period from 1980 to 1990 enrolled full time in American universities. If you didn't smoke pot back then, there was something wrong with you. Such unsocial behavior might be construed as grounds for ruling against my suitability for parenthood. I 'fessed up. Melanie's turn. Now here's the rub. Melanie is just too well behaved. I get in trouble for spitting gum out on the street or dumping my coffee cup in a parking lot. "Civilized people don't do such things," I am constantly reminded. Melanie may have liked college, but she didn't have fun in college. In fact she left Tufts because the school was not serious enough and transferred to the University of Chicago—a school where fun goes to die.

So Melanie looked at our interrogator and said, "a little pot." Stony silence. "Surely, there must be further incidents of narcotics consumption in you past." That was no longer a question; we were now being confronted with demands. "No," came her reply. I should have known this was coming. Melanie stiffened her spine, stared back at the psychologist and retorted, "And just how is the related to what we are trying to accomplish in 2008?" Now it was his turn to be uncomfortable. "Well," he replied, "I'm just trying to get a measure of your emotional and psychological stability." Had this statement come from someone wearing a tie, or at least socks, I would have been impressed. As it was, Melanie simply deflected by asking if there were any more questions.

Turns out the answer was no. But, we were informed; he would be coaching our birth mother—whoever she might be—and thus this gentleman was going to be part of our lives so long as Alfred served as our attorney. Wonderful. Ok, ok, I'll can the sarcasm for a moment. In principle Alfred was doing the right thing. Many women who agree to give up a child for adoption could probably benefit from a little counseling. I know for a fact that I would be sitting in a few shrink sessions if confronted with such a profound decision. That said, it was also clear we had just acquired additional bills. Not only were we to support the birth mother, but there was also this cadre of strap-hangers charged with providing logistical support. Adoption is a marvelous option…simple it is not.

At this point we were 3 hours into Alfred's 6 hour in-take interview. Thinking we could use a break from the seemingly endless questions and Alfred's remarkably ambiguous answers, I suggested lunch. Easier said than done. While Alfred's offices are located near a major movie studio, we had missed lunch time and Melanie was not terribly impressed with the options. The food snob had spoken. Fortunately, Alfred's legal assistant had mentioned a family-run sandwich shop just one block away. Lunch, like breakfast, is a pass in my book. In this case, however, we needed a few minutes away from the confines of Alfred's dusty library/conference room. (The law books on those shelves hadn't been moved in years…a large collection of California statutes that appeared intended to impress clients more than actually guide decision-making.)

Despite our misgivings about Alfred's tardiness and deliberate ambiguity about costs, we agreed to proceed. The one option working in his favor—when we had mentioned our desire to adopt a child of mixed or African-American heritage the wait times had dropped from a year to less than 6 months. As neither of us were getting any younger—I want to attend my daughter's high school graduation without use of a walker or wheelchair—the shorter wait times were a real plus. Alfred also expressed a willingness to shave $10,000 off his costs if we were willing to adopt such a child.

You read that correctly. The attorney was willing to reduce his costs if we wanted to adopt a child of mixed or African-American heritage. Why? My assumption, and I am not alone in reaching this conclusion, adoption agencies and associated attorneys can not appear to be discriminatory—even if a majority of their clients are only interested in a white child. To increase the odds of placing these "less desirable" children, Alfred—and likely other attorneys—simply reduce the cost. I told you this is a business with a distinct focus on bottom lines and profit.

I would be lying if I said we didn't discuss the savings. But it was never a factor in our final decision. We simply wanted to start a family, and if our open-minded approach to the color of our child lowered the final cost, great. As you will see, in the end money was not the issue. But in May 2008 we were still novices and were more delighted with the idea of finding a daughter by Christmas than saving a few dollars. Alfred had simply offered an option that made up for some of his warts.

Keeping all this in mind, we walked back into the office prepared for another round of mind-number sessions. Low and behold, Alfred was nowhere to be found, but his legal assistant had placed a TV and VCR on the conference table. "Watch this and let me know if you have any further questions." The screen flickered on and there—15 years younger and 25 pounds lighter—sat Alfred. For the next 20 minutes we were lulled into submission with the most boring video I have ever managed to stay awake through. It was, quite honestly, the Cliff Notes version of the 3 hours we had just survived. Argh.

The grainy video came to an end and Alfred suddenly appeared again in person. "Any questions?" Seeing none, he pulled out a folder with all the appropriate contracts and documentation. Fifteen pages of signatures and a check for $5,000 later, we were free to go. The hunt for our daughter was about to commence.

Chapter III
Home Sweet Home

...it is less trouble and more satisfaction to bury two families than to select and equip a home for one.

—*Mark Twain*

I am not a "stuff" person. Having managed to move almost every 24 months over the last 18 years, I simply see little purpose in cluttering one's life with a mountain of possessions. My philosophy can be boiled down to buy a book, read same, and then give it away. The result, when I moved to Washington from Hawaii my "household" possessions consisted of a motorcycle and three suitcases filled with cloths...that's it. Needless to say, that is no longer the case.

Melanie has some very different thoughts on stuff. As best I can tell she has retained every book she's ever purchased, and clearly believes a home should be furnished with something more than a futon and a couple of stools parked in front of a kitchen counter. (Hey, at least I wasn't eating while standing over the sink—I'm not a complete barbarian.) When we first met, she lived in a very fully furnished two bedroom house that offered about a thousand feet of living space. My lack of possessions was a real plus, as there would have been no place to put them.

In November 2007, we purchased a "newer" home about a block and a half from the old place. New is a relative term. The old house had been constructed in 1850; the new one went up in 1890. The big difference? The new house has three bedrooms, three and half baths, and a full basement. Total living space, about 2,000 square feet. Now a few of you already know what happened when we moved. The rest of you are about to find out.

First, a comment on moving. Melanie was in no real rush to leave the old house. She had lived there for almost 10 years and was partial to the neighbors and neighborhood. As a result she subscribed to the gradual move theory. That is, I was directed to pack boxes and then move them via my station wagon to the new house. I have a Subaru Outback—not a huge car and the number of boxes in each trip was limited to a handful. Despite my persistence in moving at least two carloads each day, at the end of three weeks I was still coming home to more packing.

Furthermore, it was not unusual for me to discover that closets I thought had been emptied would magically restock—with more stuff. This went on for about a month and a half, before we finally reached the stage of clearing out the furniture. One U-Haul and a couple of friends later, we were done. Sort of. You see, once the old furniture went in the new house Melanie decided it was time to upgrade. I told you some readers already knew where this was heading…to the furniture store.

But not just any furniture store. We had to shop at Pierre Dux. For the uninitiated, Pierre Dux is a stuffy chain of fabric and French furniture shops where the clerks drink tea with their pinky appropriately lifted from the cup. The stores apparently come with an automatic floral scent, and the ladies who run them inevitably have a foreign accent—preferably from somewhere in "old Europe." Not exactly my idea of a hot date, but when directed to help select a couch and chairs for the living room I know my role as well as the next guy. "Yes dear, that would look wonderful in blue with white lace doilies."

That's not fair. Melanie did not want doilies. She did, however, have this vision of decorating our home in a French provincial style. Full disclosure, I had no damn idea what she was talking

Adopting Ainsley

about. I can identify motorcycle makes and models from a half mile away. I'm pretty good at determining sailboat manufactures. And, I do a decent job sorting lumber at the hardware store. Furniture styles are a whole different story. I had visions of over-stuffed chairs with ornate carvings and delicate trim. The kind of stuff you can look at, but are afraid to sit on.

I need not have been worried. Turns out French provincial is user friendly. Simple, clean lines in varnished oak. The coach is actually nap worthy, and the fabrics are bright—lots of red, blue, and yellow. The only down side, the prints are heavy on the pastoral scenery and there is a curious fascination with chickens. That's right, chickens. I once counted the number of pillows or other items we own with chickens on them. I stopped when the collection accounted for all my fingers and toes....and I still was on the first floor. (Not to be outdone, I eventually bought a five-foot tall metal rooster assembled by a Mexican artist and planted him in the front yard. The neighbors were slightly appalled, but now no one has a hard time identifying our house.)

It took six months, but when Melanie was finished we had decorated the entire house in this manner. With one exception, the baby's room. Back to my stuff philosophy. I know babies don't automatically come with "stuff," but I am aware of the fact they seem to attract it. So I wasn't terribly worried by the absence of objects in the baby's future room. Rather, I suspected the required accoutrements would all appear in good time.

Melanie was not buying my argument. Having sat down with Alfred, she now assumed we needed to get cracking on the job of outfitting the baby's room. As far as I was concerned, no problem—I'd driven past a veritable ocean of baby stores in northern Virginia, and then there was always K-mart, Wal-mart, or IKEA. Right. As soon as those ingenious ideas passed from my lips I knew I was in trouble. Melanie just looked at me as though I had taken up a foreign language—one that only made sense to the speaker.

Eric C Anderson

"IKEA?" she asked, "surely you must be kidding." Well, no, but I've learned there are times to transmit and times to receive. This was definitely a "receive" moment. "Our daughter is not growing up on IKEA furniture—and Wal-mart is out, out, out." (Being a dedicated liberal, Melanie has issues with Wal-mart…I personally find their stock to be a nice counter-cyclical in our investment portfolio, but like I said, there are times to transmit and times to receive.) That's how I found myself scouring the internet for cribs.

The same thing occurred, by the way, when it came time to discuss wall decorations, a carpet, and rocking chair for the baby's room. I would offer a suggestion, and Melanie would roll her eyes. Eventually she would tell me what was going to happen, but in the interim I was offered the opportunity to at least winnow down choices by throwing out recommendations. The conversations would go like this. Me, "How about a carpet with stars or funny shapes in blue." Melanie, "No, I'm still looking." Me, "How about hanging letters on the wall?" Melanie, "No, I'm still looking." Me, "How about a simple wood rocker?" Melanie, "No, I'm still looking."

So what did we land up with? The carpet is pink with white polka dots. The walls are yellow with antique metal stars painted in different colors. And the rocker? The rocker is an over-stuffed, apple-green glider with an ottoman. The room looks good and the chair is comfortable, but now I'm afraid to go in out of fear something will get dirty. It took the dog and I weeks to get used to this pristine new environment. Hopefully, the child won't be a messy baby. I'm not sure how one gets milk or other baby excretions off white polka dots that are set on a pink background. (In hindsight, I can forthrightly declare the answer is, you don't…live with the stains, worse things are going to happen…trust me.)

So much for the easy stuff. The real challenge came in selecting a crib and dresser. Now I realize cribs are mandatory furnishing for anyone expecting a small child. And I know said item has to be safe and be constructed like a prison cell so one has a place to confine the little angels once they've driven you nuts. What I don't understand is why cribs need to cost so much. This is a piece of furniture that, if you're lucky, will have about an 18-24 month life span. After that point the kids are either too heavy to be hoisted over the crib walls, or they have learned to escape and it's better to have them fall off a bed than tumble from the top of their former cell.

I tried to make this point on multiple occasions—all to no avail. Melanie was searching for the perfect crib. You know, the one that went well with yellow walls, a pink carpet, and apple-green over-stuffed glider. That meant brown was out, black was out, and natural finish was deemed just plain unthinkable. It was white, or nothing. But not just any white, it had to be antique white and the crib had to blend with the rest of our French provincial furniture. I'm thinking the child will be sleeping on the floor long before this set of criteria is ever satisfactorily matched.

I was wrong. Melanie—who wrinkles her nose at my Wal-Mart suggestions—is like many older well-to-do parents in our demographic group and initially spent hours poring over upscale baby furniture catalogs. Luckily, she also expended more than a few days with books dedicated to child safety—the *Consumer Reports* of cribs if you will. This is what apparently saved us from Pottery Barn and Restoration Hardware. The child was to be spared the floor, but only because we had expanded the shopping universe.

Out of the blue Melanie suggested a trip to Buy-Buy Baby—the Wal-mart of baby-related goods. If you have infant needs—aside from the child itself—Buy-Buy Baby is the place for you. You name it, they have it. The place could only improved by adding a television and stock of cold beer so dads can watch football games while moms pick through cute baby clothes and decide on sheet colors. Yup, white sheets are apparently passé, now one has to have patterns and hues of red, yellow, and blue. (I clearly led a deprived childhood—we were lucky to even have sheets, less colored sheets.

My mother would have been happy to just have us parked in sleeping bags. The logic? Sleeping bags are easy to clean up….and there's no making the bed.)

Anyway, here we are at Buy-Buy Baby looking at cribs….for three hours. I'm a patient guy, but three hours of furniture shopping will drive even me nuts. "What do you think of this one, Dear?" "No, wrong white." "What about this one?" "No, wrong shape." And so on…until, finally in desperation I leaned up on one of the more tucked away models. "That one!" Success, but this was only step one.

Cribs, it turns out, don't come with mattresses. That you have to purchase separately. I know something about mattress purchases. When we replaced the mattress in our bedroom we shopped by spending several hours testing models at a local store. Not a bad job. You bring a newspaper and comfortable pillow…and then just flop on one bed after another. I'll go mattress shopping any time. The naps are great. The same is not true for crib mattresses. As with adult options, there are multiple choices—only you can't ask the intended recipient to rest test during the selection process.

What happens instead? You ask the sales clerk. Who will then inform you that some models are two-sided—hard on one side for newborns…then flip over for softer sleeping as child develops—others have springs, and yet a third group are filled with memory foam. What a scam. Babies, as we all know, will sleep just about anywhere. Why they need a $200 mattress is beyond me. Now I have to be honest, we have a mattress in Ainsley's crib, but I sure don't remember what we selected, or why. By the time I had loaded the mattress into the shopping cart Melanie had focused on sheet selection. Having yellow, polka-dotted sheets was far more important than springs, foam, or two-sided mattresses—really, what is the matter with my priorities.

Oh, one other little detail about purchasing a crib. They do not come assembled and the box does not fit in an ordinary car.

Adopting Ainsley

Quite frankly, the box probably doesn't fit in most mini-vans. So there I was, in a driving rain, lashing the crib to the roof of my Subaru, wondering how long it was going to take to assemble this Rube Goldberg invention. I am not easily intimidated by such tasks, there's a full woodshop in the basement. But the crib had more pieces and parts than a fully disassembled child's bike on the night before Christmas. Took me three hours and a full tool box to complete the mission. I hope Ainsley likes the crib, I'm not sure I can take the thing back apart without using saws or a lot of brute force.

This left us with just one more item. The dresser. Like cribs, children's dressers are horribly overpriced and typically will not meet with Melanie's approval. "Too tall," "too wide," or "too modern" were all refrains I could soon recite without notice. Wal-Mart was out, IKEA would never happen, and Pierre Dux simply didn't carry this kind of furnishing. In desperation I suggested used furniture shops. The first three stops didn't pan out…the fourth, Salvation Army, was more promising. There, in the back of the shop, hidden from site because of its condition, was the dresser Melanie was seeking—so long as Eric was willing to repair, refurbish, and change the color.

So there I was, for the second time, loading furniture onto the car in the driving rain. I'm not sure what the previous owners used this dresser for. I suspect it was storing bricks. To repair the damn thing I had to completely take it apart. Then glue it back together and begin sanding. Three days later the dresser was varnished inside and out—and then coated with a great antique white finish. The original purchase price was a hundred bucks. The sandpaper, varnish, paint and my time probably amounted to several times that—but no one said adopting was cheap or easy.

That took care of the baby's room. With all the pink, yellow and green it looked appropriately cheerful and ready for other adult approval. See, here's the trick. Mothers spend an inordinate amount of time decorating the baby's room as a means of impressing other mothers. Tell me the number of men you know who have actually asked to be given a tour of the baby's room. And the babies really don't care. According to the medical folks the kids can barely see, and they have no idea what they're looking at anyway. You could place a baby in a large cardboard box, and it would be happy as long as food and diaper changes were delivered in a timely fashion.

Mothers, on the other hand, really get into this. I'm sure there is an informal gossip cycle that brutally evaluates how each child's room is decorated. I can hear the conversation now. In a disapproving tone someone asks, "Did you see what Ms. X did with her baby's room?" "Yes," comes the reply, "it's ghastly. Imagine having to grow up in a space that is painted white and only has normally framed pictures on the wall." "And that carpet, really, no one should let their child mature in a space that does not have a rug with educational shapes." Sigh, I had such a deprived childhood. It's really amazing that I can actually read and write at this stage in my career.

Oh, that brings me to the second baby-related item that apparently causes mother angst and envy. Strollers. Unlike a crib, I actually understand the need for a stroller. It is impossible to leave the house without a stroller…and I am not wearing one of those Baby Bjorn contraptions. First, you look silly with a baby hanging off your chest with its arms inevitability waving about like some uncontrollable alien. Second, people give you dirty looks when the smoke from my cigar inevitably drifts down over the attached infant.

Nope give me a stroller any day. Strollers can be used to lug child, the required collection of diapers and bottles, and make for great tool transport devices when wandering about the hardware store. Furthermore, there is something respectable about a man who is pushing a stroller while smoking a cigar and walking the dog. Well, perhaps respectable is too strong a word. Suffice it to say I get fewer dirty looks with the baby in a stroller while enjoying my cigar than I did in the Baby Bjorn situation. My son spent most of his first two years of life stowed in such rolling contraptions…and seems none the worse for wear.

I would also note his strollers never cost more than 50 dollars. In fact, a majority cost exactly $19.99. That's how much K-mart used to charge for one of the rapid fold, light weight "umbrella" strollers. Sure, they may not be the most sturdy transportation device. And the canvas seats inevitably assume this permanent dirty look 20 minutes after purchase. Who cares? They meet a basic need in a cheap and reliable manner. Lose one, no sweat. Break one, no sweat. Put it in the car, no sweat.

Now, let's recall Melanie's approach to hotels, restaurants, and household furnishing. We don't own an umbrella stroller. (But I am planning to hide one in the back of my station wagon in the near future.) We own a stroller that will double as my wheelchair in another 20 years. It has been crash tested and the airbags deploy with minimal damage to bystanders. It also weighs something close to 50 pounds and folds down to the size of two fully laden golf bags. Great device if you don't need to go down steps (you'll be pulled off balance) or actually place the thing in the back of any vehicle outside a pickup truck.

The selling point? It's the model of choice on Capitol Hill. But I'm getting ahead of myself. Back to prices. Strollers are not cheap. The top of the line Bugaboo comes in at nearly $1,000 and it's not alone. One of the fancier contraptions is called the Orbit Infant System. For a mere $900 you have a stroller with a detachable base and a whole line of upgrades. Think I'm kidding? Here's how the manufacturer describes this thing:

> *The Orbit Infant System is the world's first upgradeable travel system. The Orbit Infant System "starter kit" includes everything you need for your newborn. You can easily dock and rotate your Infant Car*

Eric C Anderson

> *Seat onto the stroller chassis or base in the car. The stroller frame can fold with one hand and the base can be easily installed properly with the turn of a knob. The Orbit Infant System offers a safe and secure car seat that can be made into an ergonomic, premium travel system. As you baby grows up, you can continue to use your stroller and base with other Orbit seats.*

I told you things are getting out hand in stroller land. Since when did strollers have "docking" options or suggest the child needs to be placed in an "ergonomic" position? Not only will children sleep anywhere, they do so in positions that would cause you or me to wake up with permanent nerve and back damage. No infant needs an "ergonomic premium travel system." All this stuff is simply designed to provide parental bragging rights.

So we avoided the Bugaboo and the Orbit Infant System. Melanie instead steered us into Phil and Ted's Classic Stroller. Not sure why they use the word "classic" to describe this model. For one thing there is no wicker or wood to be found on the stroller. Secondly, when I think of a classic I'm thinking basic and inexpensive. This is neither. Phil and Ted's Classic Stroller is all space-age materials with a window sticker price of $400. That's more than I paid for my first two cars and my first motorcycle.

The real trick to Phil and Ted's game is the accessories. Once you have the stroller, you just *must* have the accessories. These include: a storm cover, a sun cover, a hang bag, saddle bags, a sleeping bag, and a fleece lined "buggy bunny." Oh, I forgot, you can also purchase a second seat that attaches behind and below the primary stroller occupant. The total cost for all these goodies? Another 350 bucks. I'll admit right now, we have most of the accessories—I'm still waiting for the saddle bags. I suspect the only deterrent is their color. All the other stuff comes in a fire-engine red that matches the stroller. The saddle bags are grey—Melanie will never go for that.

Adopting Ainsley

So now the room is ready, the *de rigueur* transportation device has been acquired, and we have even purchased a box of diapers. All we need now is the baby…time for Alfred to begin working his magic. We're getting impatient and Melanie is out of nesting tasks that had kept her preoccupied. Going to the park has become an exercise in watching other parents with toddlers and wondering when we would be chasing our own over-dressed munchkin.

Chapter IV
Tucson or Bust

I was seldom able to see an opportunity until it had ceased to be one.

—Mark Twain

Allow me to open with a truism, no adoption opportunity will arise until one has other plans in hand—usually a long-awaited vacation. With the house now readied, the crib properly dressed, and diapers purchased, we commenced the process of awaiting "the call." Alfred had every number we could think of…including close associates…and Melanie had taken to placing her blackberry on vibrate when we went to a movie just in case news came at an inopportune moment. All to no avail. June came and went. July was its usual sticky unpleasantness, and August was promising to offer more of the same. Seeking to avoid the worst of August—the 90 degree-90 percent humidity dog days—we scheduled a trip to San Francisco.

Melanie infrequently has to travel for work. These adventures usually focus on conferences or fund-raising—not her favorite events—but typically take place somewhere pleasant like San Diego, New York or Miami. In this case, she was slated for a conference in San Francisco and we decided I would meet her there for a few days of rest and relaxation once the conference was over. Good intentions—about to be rent asunder.

At about 6 pm on the second day of Melanie's conference the phone rang at home in Washington. Figuring it was my lovely wife calling to share the day's news, I answered with a cheery, "Hello Dear." You can imagine my surprise upon hearing Alfred's voice on the other end of the line. "I have an adoption opportunity for you in Tucson." "Tucson?" I replied. "Yes," Alfred continued, "Tucson…and the mother is in labor right now." Wow!

Alfred went on to explain the birth mother was a Native American and the birth father was of African-American heritage. He told me nothing else, except he believed the mother was prepared to place the child for adoption pending identification of a suitable family. Alfred declared he needed an answer from us in the next 30 minutes or he would contact the next couple on his list. All good news as far as I was concerned; there was just one drawback, I could not make a decision without talking to Melanie.

Ever try to reach someone in a hurry, only to be frustrated at every turn? Melanie is a Blackberry addict, she does not, however, feel overly inclined to actually use the telephone option on those infernal gadgets. This is particularly true when she is traveling or attending conferences or meetings. I, on the other hand, have no interest in text messaging or continual access to my email—and so depend on verbal communication. As you have already probably surmised, this made the 30 minute rule more than a little stressful.

Now, I might not be the brightest guy, but I do know most hotels are capable of locating guests attending meetings in their facilities. Most hotels. In this case, calling the front desk was nothing more than an exercise in futility. "Good evening, I am trying to reach a guest attending the Momentum conference." The reply, "what conference?" "The Momentum conference." The reply, "never heard of it." Never mind that 200 or so leaders of this country's largest progressive organizations had taken over the hotel and were freely mingling in the hotel's ballrooms, restaurants and bars. As best I could tell, the desk clerk just didn't want to be bothered…the great American service sector at work.

So I called the hotel switchboard. "Could I be connected with Ms. Melanie Sloan?" "Who?" "Melanie Sloan." "Who?" "M-e-l-a-n-i-e S-l-o-a-n." "Oh, you mean Melanie Sloan?" Sigh, "Yes." "Hold on,

I'll connect you with her room." Another deep sigh on my end of the line.

"My wife is not in her room, could you please page her in the conference center?" "I'm sorry sir, but we have a meeting taking place there—you will have to contact the front desk for bell service." An even deeper sigh from me...great, the hotel switchboard knows about the conference, but the mouth breathers actually tasked with greeting these guests were completely out of the loop. It's moments like this that cause me to understand why the captains of American industry have farmed out their customer service centers. At least the kids working in India's phone-bank sweat shops sound interested in my problems. The same certainly could not be said of the young lady currently on the other end of the line.

Completely frustrated with this clown act, I chose the old fashioned route. I fired up the laptop and sent an email. So much for instant communication and microwave towers—I was back to the 21st century equivalent of the telegram, now I had to hope Melanie was in her usual Blackberry addict mode.

Thirty seconds later the phone rang. Melanie! Nope, Alfred. "Do you have an answer for me yet?" "Alfred, it's only been twenty minutes." Long pause from L.A., "Look, we can't wait much longer." I heard my cell phone ring. "Alfred, I have to go, Melanie is dialing back in...set up a conference call." Leaving these words of wisdom for the attorney, I grabbed the cell phone call from my wife.

In rapid fire succession I explained what I knew of the situation, and told her Alfred was planning to fill in the details via a conference call. I should have known that answer was not going to satisfy my in-residence attorney. "Boy or girl?" "I don't know." "Healthy or issues?" "I don't know, dear." "Mother's prenatal care and drug use?" "Dear, I still don't know...let's get Alfred on the line and have him provide some answers." That response earned me a "what took you so long to contact me?" And then the line went dead—Melanie was already calling Alfred, I'd just have to catch up on another line.

For the first time that evening America's communication system didn't fail me. In less than five minutes I was dialed into the conference call where Melanie was grilling Alfred. Did I mention adopting can be nerve wracking? This really was the hard part. Over the course of a 15 minute cryptic conversation we were expected to make a decision about flying across the country and potentially adding a family member who would forever change our lives. I don't think it's possible to ask enough questions in such a situation—fortunately, Melanie clearly was operating in the same mode. Alfred, however, was apparently already planning for happy hour. To say the least he was uninformed—at worst, he was downright deceptive.

Apparently the young lady in question—an 18 year-old freshman at the University of Arizona—had only been in contact with his office for the last 24-36 hours. No medical or psychological screening had been done, and her answers to his multi-page application form could be graciously described as less than complete. (A polite way of saying they were nonexistent.) Nonetheless, Alfred was relatively sure she wanted to proceed with the adoption and he counseled we fly out to meet with the birth mother as soon as possible. Melanie and I huddled as best one can over 3,000 mile-long phone connection and decided to wait until the baby had been born before launching into a mad-dash scramble.

The next morning, Alfred informed us the young lady had given birth to a healthy baby girl. That answered all of Melanie's questions in one fell swoop. "Re-pack your bags, we're headed for Tucson." Ok, so out goes the sailing gear in and goes the shorts and a swimsuit—I know they have pools in the desert, they are certainly less prevalent in chilly San Francisco. Simple enough. Alas, we still had one large problem—we had yet to finish our home study.

A home study is another hurdle adoptive parents must clear as a result of their inability to conceive in the privacy of one's own bedroom. In many ways, the home study is very similar to the paperwork demanded for an over-seas adoption—only in this case you have an opportunity to enrich a local business. Alfred assured us this could be done in a relatively rapid manner, and, besides, because the mother was Native American, we weren't leaving Arizona in anything less than 10 days. Ten days! Yup. Seems the states have all enacted laws intended to protect American Indians from child-stealing adoptive parents. In Arizona that meant a 10-day cooling off period, while the attorneys racked up billing hours filling out forms in triplicate. Ah well, beggars can't be choosers.

One thing was certain; we were going to have to get to Tucson in short order and figure out how to complete a home study post haste. Melanie reminded me the family who had recommended Alfred to us also stepped into a last-minute adoption, so the agency that had completed their home study might be a good choice. She got on the phone and found the agency's number. I agreed to get the process going while Melanie ditched her conference and took off for Tucson.

Before we go forward, let's spend a moment on this home study malarkey. According to the U.S. government, "The laws of every State and the District of Columbia require all prospective adoptive parents (no matter how they intend to adopt) participate in a home study." The bureaucrats in Washington go on to contend, "This process has three purposes: to educate and prepare the adoptive family for adoption, to gather information about the prospective parents that will help a social worker match the family with a child whose needs they can meet, and to evaluate the fitness of the adoptive family."

Eric C Anderson

The rest of the story works like this. The home studies are typically accomplished by private agencies who charge between one and two thousand dollars for the privilege of making you fill out endless forms and suffer through a barrage of ridiculous questions. These studies are largely accomplished by women serving as the second bread winner—and are by no means authoritative or correct. Instead, they result in a 10 page, poorly written paper that ultimately concludes you are prepared to be adoptive parents...unless you lit a bong in front of the "social worker" or actually do live in a one bedroom mobile home.

So what is in the report? Here's a typical sample:

- **Health and income**—are you going to live long enough to raise the child and not have the infant become a ward of the state
- **Family background**—an idealized descriptions of your childhood, how you were parented, past and current relationships with parents and siblings...leave off the part about your mother telling you to go play in traffic
- **Education/employment**—Did you actually finish high school and have you been able to hold down gainful employment since that memorable occasion
- **Relationships**—wherein you inform the social worker that of course you and your significant other never argue or fight...that's something only other people do....
- **Daily life**—get out of bed, take shower, go to office, eat dinner, watch TV...fall asleep at 10 and then repeat... oh, you should have some respectable hobbies like gardening or sports, but I don't recommend mentioning the beer can collection
- **Parenting**—how you have adversely impacted other small children's lives
- **Neighborhood**—Honest, expensive alarm system, big dog, and bars on the windows are not indicative of a problem
- **Religion**—I think there are churches, etcetera within 5-10 miles

- **Feelings about/readiness for adoption**—I about gagged on this one, why do you think we are allowing you in our home to ask all these intrusive questions?
- **Approval/recommendation**—Did the check you wrote to pay for this fiction go through or bounce?

Needless to say, I was less than enthusiastic about stepping through this informal interrogation once again. To make matters worse, the agency Melanie had selected was located in Northern Virginia—and unpleasant drive at almost any time of day…but doubly so at rush hour, exactly when I was dispatched in their direction. Seeking to make the best of a bad situation, I ignored the ominous dark clouds and fired up the bike. Why wait in traffic when you can run the white line right up the middle of the congestion?

Conjoined, the agency in question, claims to be open from 8:30 to 5:00. Knowing I had to catch a plane no later than 3 or risk showing up in Tucson a full day after Melanie, I opted for arriving at their front door promptly at 8:30. Armed with a check written out to the tune of nineteen hundred dollars, two good cigars, and my battered cell phone, I beat feet for the destination in question at 7:30. It poured at 7:45.

There is no staying dry on a Harley when the skies open and one is rolling along at 70mph. Oh, you can dodge the big puddles and avoid the worst thunderstorms by hiding under overpasses. But as a rule, most motorcyclists worthy of that title simply choose to be manly and get wet. This is not such a horrible thing unless you need to impress someone at the other end of your adventure. In such cases, I have discovered wet motorcyclists are a great way to turn off dates, cause extra security guards to follow you around in banks, and generally dismay current or would-be employers. I showed up at Conjoined soaked…only to find the doors locked and the lights out. Seems 8:30 in the adoption world actually means something about 30 minutes later than it does for those of us condemned to live in reality. (I should have learned this lesson after our first meeting with Alfred...suffice it to say I make no claims about being a quick student.)

At 9:00 the Conjoined staff pulled into the lot. The receptionist arrived first, in a late-model Cadillac that appeared to have last visited a car wash during the Clinton administration. Obviously dismayed by the sight of me and the bike parked under the shelter of a large tree near the back of the parking lot, she glanced my direction, looked at the door to her office—clearly debated whether she could cover that distance before I was able to commence the mugging—and opted to wait for backup. At 9:10 the owner arrived...in a much newer BMW that clearly was blessed with a weekly trip to the auto beauty shop. Her car was so waxed the rain beaded before it struck the vehicle.

As it turns out, Diane—the Conjoined agency co-owner and co-founder—was nowhere as nervous as her receptionist. At first I attributed this courage to a career spent visiting strange homes. Eventually, I discovered Diane's courage was actually cluelessness. She simply didn't pay any attention to what was happening around her...a dismaying discovery given the nature of her business. In any case, she parked the car, walked up to the office door and gave a firm tug. Guess she figured the receptionist was supposed to be on time. Discovering she was locked out, Diane walked back to her car for an umbrella—I just sat and dripped under the tree.

On trip two to the office door Diane's receptionist joined her boss. Apparently this was all the backup she needed to avoid befalling a cruel fate at the hands of that strange man and his motorcycle parked at the back of the lot. I suspect that was the sentiment passed along to Diane, as there was a great deal of finger-pointing and head turning as the two of them worked at unlocking the front door. You can only imagine their "delight" when I tromped in a mere 30 seconds later.

Adopting Ainsley

The first response was a pair of dirty looks and a reach for the telephone—must have 9-1-1 on speed dial. The second look was to scan me for weapons or other obvious signs of intent to inflict bodily harm. (All this at 9:15 in the morning, I really need to pay more attention to crime stories concerning Northern Virginia… in DC one does not draw this kind of suspicion until after 11pm.) Seemingly convinced I was not there to rob the establishment, I finally drew something of a welcome from the two ladies. "What do you want?"

Whatever happened to civility and greetings like Good Morning? Particularly in businesses that depend upon you wanting to spend money with them rather than seeking alternative solutions? Not wanting to risk the wrath of Melanie by walking out the door in disgust, I opted for the fastest answer possible. "We need a home study done in less than 2 weeks and I understand you can make that happen." Silence. Apparently soaking wet men don't routinely make such requests at Conjoined.

One more time. "What I meant to say was, my wife and I are adopting a child and we have just been informed of a potential option in Tucson who was born this morning." Fluttering eyelids… finally, signs of comprehension. I was beginning to suffer a sense of *déjà vu* that had me linking this scene with the previous night's hotel desk experiences. "We can do that," Diane mumbled, "but it will cost approximately $2,000 and is nonrefundable." The receptionist nodded in accord, first signs of intelligent life on that front.

"OK," I replied.

"We need the money up front." Now the receptionist was engaged. Clearly I had to pay to play. I pulled the only dry item out of my pocket—a wallet—and placed the check on her desk. "Will this start the paperwork?" "Yes, yes," came Diane's reply. "Come up to my office and we can start the documents." Now things were beginning to look up. I wasn't going to be led away in handcuffs, dismissed for want of coat and tie, nor was I going to have to call Melanie and explain why we needed a new home study service. As far as I could tell, things were off to a promising start.

Right until I walked into Diane's office. Diane occupied a space that appeared to have been designed as a loft bedroom. The ceiling arched upward, and there was a small overlook to the reception area below. There were also piles of paper everywhere. "Please excuse the mess…we're preparing for an audit." Now I've been audited. Unless one is preparing a defense based on obfuscation, the best approach is to establish a methodical filing system that allows for near immediate location of crucial documents. That was clearly not happening at Conjoined. Furthermore, Diane seemed to be unable to locate the documents I would need to accomplish before leaving her office prepared to conduct a rapid-fire home study.

I looked at the clock, watched Diane shuffle about, and then reminded her of my situation. "I need to be on a plane for Tucson early this afternoon." "Oh, yes, you did say speed was important. I'm sorry, someone seems to have misplaced the document file." I was tempted to observe someone had apparently misplaced the entire office, but reconsidered given the situation.

After about 10 minutes of shuffling around and dialing the receptionist Diane let out a long sigh—an apparent indication she had located the paperwork in question and was prepared to begin the inquisition. She began by putting any fears I had about thoroughness immediately to rest. "According to procedures, I need to conduct three interviews with you and your wife. One must be in the home, the other two can take place here." OK, except I couldn't see Melanie being overjoyed about a trip to Vienna, Virginia—she believes crossing the Potomac requires a passport.

"Furthermore, I need to have an independent interview with you on a separate occasion." Hmmm, this was going to be complicated. "But that second interview can be done today, right after you fill out the paperwork." See, thoroughness was not exactly the order of the day…who else lets you complete two screening interviews within 15 minutes of one another? Certainly not officials charged with completing background investigations for security clearances required to enter the intelligence community. Needless to say, I was more than happy to comply.

So, what is one asked in these screening interviews intended to ensure you are ready to adopt a child? Well, your name is important—been asked that multiple times—your address is second, and then there is a five minute spiel on arrests, employment, and the state of one's marriage. It is only after this "grilling" that we eventually get around to why you want to adopt and what kind of parent you believe you will be. They should be so inquisitive when you go in to fill out marriage licenses…would have spared me a pair of very bad experiences.

The bottom line, despite my bedraggled appearance and repeated hints of impatience, Diane seemed convinced that I would make a good father. She also took a couple of pages of notes—but when I looked over her shoulder there was no telling what she had scribbled without employing the Rosetta Stone and a couple of academics who specialized in ancient Egyptian hieroglyphics. All of which prompted me to ask, "How long does it take to prepare one of these reports?" "That depends on when we get back the results of your local police and FBI background checks." Oh boy, more time with bureaucrats.

Being an analyst I could not just let this go. "Where does the finished report ultimately go?" Diane, her wig now visibly askew, looked at me as though I had just fallen off the back of the milk wagon. "To the Inter-State Compact officials, where else would it go?" The Inter-State Compact she had me on this one…but I wasn't going to hang around to await an explanation—that's why they invented the Internet. Plus, I had a plane to catch and still lacked tickets, packed luggage, and still needed to make my way back to Washington. The Inter-State Compact could wait.

I bid Diane and her much-relieved receptionist adieu and headed for the parking lot. The clock on her wall said 11:00, my wife had made threatening comments about being on a plane no later than 2, this was going to be an exercise in rapid transportation. Comfort and convenience were out—now I was simply grasping for straws and hoping I could make it to one of our inconvenient airports on time to miss a severe tongue-lashing from my significant other.

Chapter V
Miraculous Virgin Conception

It is not immoral to create the human species—with or without ceremony.
—*Mark Twain*

I can distinctly recall a time when airline reservations had to be done through a travel agent or in person. In the worst case, one could show up at an airport and attempt to purchase a ticket at the front desk—but only if cost was not a consideration. No more. It is now possible to find a flight and acquire a reasonably priced boarding pass from the comfort of one's home. It is also possible to accomplish this feat within 2 hours of take off...I know, I've done it.

My departure from the Conjoined parking lot was a bit of a thing to behold. Having never been a fan of stock Harleys—who wants the environmentally friendly exhaust system or the miserly factory carburetor?—I ride a motorcycle that generates about 40 more ponies than the factory originally intended. This type of tweaking is really only good for two things, running down the highway at double the double-nickel and tire spinning departures from stoplights or parking lots. If I was going to make my 2 o'clock deadline both options were going to be in order. So I left a long black streak on the asphalt outside the Conjoined office and headed for Interstate 66...the bane of Northern Virginia commuters.

For the uninitiated here's all you need to know about Interstate 66. As the only four-lane highway running west from Washington into North Virginia, it is infamous for endless traffic jams and irritated drivers. There is ceaseless talk about widening the road or further restricting access to this thoroughfare by enforcing high occupancy vehicle regulations. To date, neither has happened and we all cringe when told a particular destination is best reached by employing this thin ribbon of highway. You'd think the state of Virginia and Federal government could do better—you'd be wrong.

Knowing I was apt to run into traffic that could have devastating consequences for my flight plans, I chose the option only available to motorcycles…straddle the white dashed lines running between the creeping automobiles. This tactic works on almost every occasion, so long as one keeps an eye out for law enforcement. Virginia—unlike California—does not smile upon such antics, and I could ill-afford a time-wasting conversation about my chosen mode of transportation. So I lit the throttle and pretended I was invisible, or at least obscured behind the customary cloud of cigar smoke that accompanies any trip on the motorcycle. You know what? It worked.

I made to the house in less than 35 minutes, a new personal best. Now to make that flight reservation, pack the suitcase, and head for the airport. As best I could tell that all had to be accomplished in the next 20 minutes, or my name was mud and no home study was going to be able to explain my demise caused by arriving in Tucson 36 hours after Melanie had set foot on the ground. Come on internet, don't fail me now.

In the first five minutes of desperate web browsing I came to the following none-too-stunning conclusions: (1) It is impossible to fly from Washington DC to Tucson nonstop; (2) I was going to be driving to Dulles or paying a fortune for the luxury of traveling to Arizona; (3) There is no logic to airline ticket pricing—how is it possible for the cost of the same one-way trip to range between $400 and $900? Keep in mind this price range was for seats in the back of the bus…I didn't even bother to look at options that included my actually being provided leg room and a "free" tuna

Adopting Ainsley

fish sandwich. With no time to dither, I opted for the $400 ticket. Southwest Airlines here I come.

But only after I jammed some clothing in a suitcase. At least on this front I was in luck. My career, as humble as it may be, has been marked by endless road trips. As a result, I never pack the night before I travel. Admittedly, this can have downsides, like forgetting underwear or a toothbrush. The advantage, however, is avoiding over packing. If you only have 20 minutes to select clothing and a few books you don't debate the green or brown socks—white will do and the current bedside reading is just fine until one arrives at the final destination. (This is perhaps a too revealing observation—many people believe white socks are for kids and rednecks, they're not—and almost all of us think the bedside books are a better option than television. Who are you kidding? I wake up more often with a book on my face that I probably should admit.)

In this case 20 minutes to pack would have been a luxury; I was down to 10 and still needed to jump in the shower. Thinking we might be stuck in Tucson for up to 10 days I went for the logical approach—gym clothes, two pair of shorts, a handful of BVDs, and the flip-flops. All logical choices as far as I could tell. Particularly since there seemed a high probability I would be sitting in a hotel room of some type seeking to satisfy a starving baby. Even I know such an occupation does not require long pants and creased shirts. Who is going to complain? Certainly not the newborn and Melanie is already used to my wayward home attire.

That left me amusing myself. In August 2008, I was in the midst of writing a book on sovereign wealth funds. Educated in the days when one actually went to a library and checked out books and magazines, I am really only able to process complex information when it appears in a printed format. This meant I had somewhere in the vicinity of 5,000 articles or essays stowed in a cabinet in our dining room. Oh, the material was sorted into appropriately labeled folders, but that still meant I needed to grab 10 pounds of paper and the laptop before walking out the door—that filled the next 8 minutes of my packing. On to the shower.

As members of the Army and Navy can tell you, it is possible to take a shower in two minutes if you don't mind cold water and don't use much soap. I was in the Air Force, where the golf courses are manicured, the hotels have cable TV, and showers are warm. Not today. Throwing my still soaked cloths in the hamper, I dashed through the coldest shower of my adult life and grabbed a clean pair of jeans and a t-shirt. Wallet and keys in hand, I picked up the roll-on and briefcase and headed out the door. Good thing the dog was in daycare—I don't think I could have left enough food or water on the floor to tide her over…and I certainly had no time left to play "run the pooch about" games.

So now its 12:45 and my flight is at 2:10. My flight is out of Dulles and, alas, I must again get on Highway 66…there is no god. But for once the planets were aligned in my favor. Traffic was rolling at 70mph—the Washington area commuter's favorite speed when the law is not about—and the foul weather had blown through. A perfect combination for a dash to the airport.

As I've previously mentioned, Dulles International Airport is located 26 miles outside the nation's capitol. While there is no realistic public transportation serving the airport, it sits at the end of a 12 mile-long limited access road. Constructed literally in the median of a six lane toll way, this access road is restricted to airport traffic and tends to be congestion free. There is one significant drawback to employing this option—the state of Virginia seems to believe this is the best place to park law enforcement officers who are intent on writing speeding tickets. To make matters worse, the speed limit on this access road is 55mph—a decision that seems largely intended to abet collection of speeding fines from people seeking to get in and out of Dulles as quickly as possible. Sigh, set the speed control at 60mph and try to avoid the temptation to

Adopting Ainsley

override the car's brain. Best not to add a hundred and fifty dollar speeding ticket onto an already expensive airline bill.

This precaution gets me to Dulles at 1:20. I'm still not sweating the flight...primarily because ignorance is bliss. Little did I realize the buses serving long-term parking are on a 15 minute rotation. By the time I make the terminal at 1:38 frazzled would be a much better description of my condition. I still owe the security guards and ticket agents a thank you note. A bit of desperate pleading won me rights to cut to the front of the line at the check-in counter and at security. Even more fortuitously, my flight was actually departing from the main terminal...no trundling about the tarmac on Dulles' land-bound space shuttle fleet.

Needless to say, I was the last one on the plane. Ever flown on Southwest? It's an interesting experience. The airline has no reserved seats and the crew is encouraged to be...hmmm...I'll stick with eccentric. This means they can be "humorous" when trying to squeeze the skinny white guy in between the two largest women on the flight. Suffice it to say the ladies were not moving and the crew's offer to get out the WD-40 was not helping. I flew the leg to Chicago's Midway airport with my Ipod turned on full volume to avoid the negative consequences of this initial encounter. Rule One, never show up late for a Southwest Flight.

Lesson two, avoid Midway airport. Midway is the poor second cousin for O'Hare International Airport. It is famous for having a brick wall at one end of the runway, and little else. The wall, as it turns out, does make Midway memorable for passengers. In order to avoid unsightly collisions with the immobile object pilots land at Midway and immediate slam on the breaks. Needless to say, objects in the overhead and in the seats next to you are abruptly shifted as a result. This once again set off my temporary traveling companions and reminded me to never violate Rule One.

So now I'm about a third of the way to Tucson and realize it would be a good idea to have something to eat—for the first time today. While airports are never listed as highly recommended dining spots, Midway appears intent on maintaining a mediocre reputation. I "dined" on pretzels and beer—the meal of champions, or at least those of us unfortunate enough to be stuck in the great cog that is America's service-less airline industry. I used to complain about airline food—now I miss it.

My flight from Midway to Tucson was uneventful...mostly. Recall I mentioned the Southwest crews can be eccentric? Well after "team reciting" flight safety procedures, the cabin attendants chose to distribute the complimentary peanuts in a unique manner. Immediate after takeoff, when the plane was in a steep climb, they dumped the box of individual peanut servings in the middle of the aisle and let gravity do the rest. We all eventually received a share, but were a bit concerned about how they were planning to serve the soda and coffee. Roll the cans and slide the hotpots?

Tucson.

I made it into Tucson at 10pm. Upon checking my voice mail I discovered Melanie had already made a car reservation and that all I needed to do was locate the appropriate rental office. Not a hard task in the nearly empty terminal, and the desk was actually manned and helpful. What they did not do, however, is warn me about the consequences of renting the cheapest car on the lot. When I walked out to the parking lot and found a bright yellow Chevy Cobalt, my heart sank. There are many reasons the U.S. taxpayer became a part owner of General Motors—the Chevy Cobalt is one of them.

Intended to draw first-time buyers with its low price, sporty appearance, and flashy colors, the Cobalt is best considered as an option for one's teenager who refuses the family station wagon. It is not a car designed to tote luggage, fit anything into the backseat or actually be able to drive in a sporty manner. It is, in short, the Chevy Vega reinvented. Oh, and did I mention the air conditioning? Seems GM designed the Cobalt's air conditioning system for Detroit—where such a "luxury" is largely unnecessary. The same is not true in Tucson, particularly in August. Even at 10pm that damn car was hot to ride in…so I opted for the next best workaround…open the windows and turn the air conditioning on full. This creates the impression of cooling, while the wind actually serves to dry a bit of the sweat running down one's back. Lovely.

I will say this of Tucson; it's easy to get around. My initial despair at finding the county hospital using the rental car standard map—an item typically best reserved for fish wrap—was unfounded. In 20 minutes I was circling the parking lot trying to figure out where to enter the sprawling complex. As I was eventually to discover, hospitals don't tend to mark the obstetrics ward as well as they advertise the emergency room. I suppose this makes sense, babies typically provide a good deal of warning about their impending arrival…somewhere in the vicinity of 9 months. That toe you just lopped off with the lawnmower is never as thoughtful.

After 10 minutes of circling I gave up and parked near what appeared the front entrance. Pulling a sport coat on over my t-shirt—no reason to alarm a birth mother with the tattoos—I did a fast shuffle into the hospital. The fact there were staff sitting at the front desk was reassuring, their directions to the delivery rooms were not. It seemed I parked as far as possible from obstetrics and was going to have to navigate a maze of hallways and locked clinics. Normally, this would not be an issue. After all, hospitals seem to be teaming with people 24 hours a day. Not this one. Once I cleared the front desk there was not a soul to be found. At least the emergency room signs were prominent and prevalent. If all else failed I could always retry the directions option upon reaching the inevitable crush of bodies that seem to permanently be parked in the vicinity of any emergency room.

For the second time that day, luck was with me. About the time I was going to fall back on plan B, a very pregnant woman waddled through a cross corridor in front of me. Recall I am an intelligence analyst. One of the first things we learn in this career field is pattern recognition. Very pregnant women in hospitals—specifically those wearing the institution's gowns—normally are kept in or near obstetrics. My thought, "follow that woman." Whoops, she just disappeared behind a locked door.

For those of you who have not been to a delivery ward or have not been there in a long, long time, a short explanation is in order. Fearful of lawsuits generated by kidnappings or miss-assigned children, hospital administrators have taken to securing delivery wards like they are some kind of medium-level prison or a storage site for nuclear weapons. (I've been in both, the analogy is not accidental…just don't ask why I was in either location.) To gain entry one has to provide identification, sign a roster, and then don a silly wrist band that apparently serves to track your location.

All of this is relatively easy to accomplish if you are the mother-to-be or her obvious significant other. (He's the one glancing about for a television or other men suffering a similar experience.) This security hurdle is much more difficult to clear by announcing "I am the prospective adoptive father." Making such a statement at the entrance to a delivery ward is best likened to shouting "I am here to steal your child—the one you have been totting around in an uncomfortable manner for the last 9 months." I could see the nurses immediately become suspicious. It didn't help I could not remember the birth mother's name, now I really was acting like a potential suspect.

About the time I was going to pull out the cell phone to plead for help from my wife, Melanie walked around the corner and spotted her wayward husband. Having clearly made acquaintances with a number of the delivery room staff over the last 8 hours, Melanie was able to quickly assure the nurses I was not a baby snatcher or misplaced psychiatric patient. Saved from a second near close encounter with law enforcement in less than 12 hours. This adoption thing was getting to be very hard on my nerves...clearly I needed to find a more conservative wardrobe for sessions involving these baby people.

Melanie was not amused by my tales of woe and/or intrigue. She had some very fundamental concerns about our potential birth mother. It turned out Melanie had been sitting with the young woman for most of the day. During that entire time period no one had called and no family members had made an appearance...all a bit strange. (I really didn't expect to hear about "Dad"...my bet was that he was long gone.) The best explanation the birth mother could offer, "My parents are at a cousin's funeral." That was quickly followed by, "My cell phone died and I forgot the charger." When Melanie offered her phone the young lady declared she "could not remember the numbers to contact her friends or family." Yup, something was wrong here.

As if this was not strange enough, the story then turned to how the birth mother had arrived at her current predicament. It seems the birth mother in question was a bit of a child protégée. She had managed to graduate from high school in three years and rack up a significant number of credits with a local community college. She had subsequently enrolled in the University of Arizona pre-med undergraduate program and moved to Tucson, about two hours from her family home. Furthermore, her academic credentials were so good a prestigious east coast school had promised her a full ride through medical school upon completing her undergraduate degree. Very impressive.

But this was where my wonderment ended. It seemed the young lady had not been aware she was pregnant until 8 months into the blessed event. Oh, I should note at this point that she clearly weighed about 100lbs soaking wet...and that was after carrying to term and delivering a healthy baby girl. So here we have a potential doctor in the making who apparently did not notice her menstrual cycle had come to an abrupt halt for over eight months and seemingly failed to be worried about the weight gain associated with this halt to the monthly cycle. No wonder our medical system is in such a disarray, the future doctors of America are not even clever enough to realize when they are pregnant…sort of makes one wonder what they will be able to do for that lingering headache you have been suffering.

Maybe that biblical story about miraculous virgin conception is not all that miraculous after all. I mean, here we are sitting in the presence of a very smart young woman who failed to notice her condition. Makes one wonder if a boy was even involved. Perhaps the Holy Ghost is up and about. Nah, I'm just being sarcastic. We were obviously not being provided the entire story. It would not be the last time.

Back to our current potential birth mother. Having provided this background, Melanie ushered me in to meet the young lady. She looked like all women who have just delivered a baby…a little disheveled and very tired. I did my best to offer an introduction and take a look at the 6 pound bundle of joy that was camped out in a rolling crib next to her bed. Despite my repeated efforts to make small talk, mom remained very quiet. I chalked this up to exhaustion and suggested we return in the morning. Everyone agreed that made good sense and we headed for the door.

We exchanged a few pleasantries with the nursing staff—always good to have at least a passing acquaintance with people we could be spending a lot of time with over the next few days. I would note that obstetric nurses must be selected for their gregarious personalities. In all our coming and going from such environments I never encountered Nurse Crotchet or her male equivalent. These people were all apparently happy to be at work—regardless of the hour—and don't seem at all fazed by the fact they are witness to countless new faces every year. There is something very reassuring about this, kind of gives one hope for humanity—no slight praise coming from someone who lives in Hollywood for Ugly People. (That would be Washington DC.)

By the time we navigated our way back to the car Melanie was filling me in with her obvious doubts about our current situation. First, she had encountered significant difficulties in contacting Alfred. Second, she was very suspicious of the story concerning the young lady's family—or absence thereof. And finally, she was dismayed by the very visible affection the birth mother was showering on this new arrival. Don't get me wrong, everyone expects a birth mother to be attached to her infant, but this affection does not bode well for a potential adoption. It becomes very hard to give up a newborn when you have bonded…even if this decision would be the best for both mother and child.

Unfortunately, there was little I could do to set Melanie's fears to rest. For the moment, the best I could offer was a sympathetic ear. And to join in the search for the place we could be calling home for the next 10 days. Ever go wandering about a new city at midnight after spending the day in a mad-dash chase? One is not at their logical best in such situations, and I am—like many men—already navigationally challenged. That is to say, I can read a map or directions. Actually translating the accumulated data into arrival at the desired destination is entirely a different story.

Fortunately the apartment complex in question was less than a mile away. So 20 minutes and three U-turns later we pulled up at the front gate. Seems, with a little help from her office, Melanie had located a service that rented furnished apartments by the week. Located on the outskirts of Tucson, the unit in question appeared to be nicely maintained and secure. Furthermore, the gentleman who ran the service was happy to go above and beyond in ensuring his customers were provided the best service. We walked into a clean, well appointed apartment where everything worked on the first try. Even Melanie was impressed…right up to the point where we crawled into bed. All I can say is never buy a cheap mattress.

Chapter VI
Disappointment in the Making

One cannot have everything the way he would like it. A man has no business to be depressed by a disappointment, anyway; he ought to make up his mind to get even.

—Mark Twain

We roused from the bed at sunrise. Sweating the uncertainty of our situation and suffering the consequence of a very uncomfortable mattress, neither of us slept well. Normally I can sleep on a floor with little difficulty; trying to accomplish this feat on a spongy surface is an entirely different matter. Years of weightlifting and assorted bad behavior...falling out of perfectly good airplanes and crossing the country on a motorcycle...do not work wonders for one's back. I shuffled to the coffee pot and then went in search of aspirin.

By the time I accomplished these essential missions Melanie had already cleared her email—the Blackberry addiction again—and managed to find us a place to eat breakfast. The hospital visiting hours began at 8 am; this meant we had two hours to kill before reappearing in the obstetrics ward...like I said; we rose with the sun, which also explained my need for at least three more cups of coffee before attempting to drive. My wife had no such limitation and was clearly searching for the cattle prod necessary to get her husband in gear.

Eric C Anderson

I should have suspected Melanie had selected a "greasy spoon" for breakfast. Every Saturday we are home in Washington we wander over to the Market Lunch, a local legend that specializes in pancakes, eggs and a friendly crowd. When that option is not available, Melanie automatically searches out a nearby facility that offers similar fair. In Tucson that option appeared in the form of an International House of Pancakes. I don't know about you, but the last time I patronized an IHOP was in college…at about 3:30 on a Sunday morning. Nothing like a stack of IHOP pancakes to help ward off a hangover. If I recall correctly, the IHOP décor and service did not warrant mention in one of my rare letters to the home front. Things have apparently not changed much. IHOP still features vinyl-clad booths that are sticky when warm and impossible to warm when cold. But the menus offer a familiar montage of breakfast options, and the coffee always comes with an extra dose of caffeine. Works for me.

Melanie had her standard fare of two eggs, hash browns, bacon and toast. I opted for a short stack and poured on the syrup. I figured the sugar would help take the edge off all the caffeine now circulating through my system. Nothing like a little diabetic shock to calm shaking hands. I wish I could say this fair was consumed over a national newspaper…but finding a copy of the *New York Times* in southern Tucson seemed about as likely as identifying a law-abiding driver in northern Virginia. This meant we were left with the *Arizona Daily Star* and *USA Today*.

This surprises some of my friends who believe I'm a news junkie, but I'm always willing to thumb through a local newspaper. This is true wherever we travel. I get a kick out of reading headlines like "Cupcake Shop to Open at Tucson's Crossroads Shopping Center" or stories about lost dogs and poorly behaved adolescents. This kind of material helps remind one that the "real" America is alive and well; the *Washington Post* never accomplishes that mission…at least as far as I'm concerned. Melanie is self-admittedly less interested in these human interest stories. Surrendering to the fact she was not going to suddenly discover a copy of the *Times*, she turned to *USA Today*.

Now, I'm old enough to recall *USA Today*'s moment of glory as Gannett's effort to establish a truly national newspaper. In those heady days the paper offered a relatively sophisticated collection of stories and commentary. No longer. Apparently written at a level considered appropriate for those of us who dropped out of school after 5th grade, *USA Today* is currently a very short step above the *National Enquirer*. Oh, I'll admit *USA Today* does seem to avoid the "aliens snatched my sister" stories that regularly appear in the *Enquirer*—but its condensed version of daily events just will not hold my interest. Melanie, on the other hand, spent a good 20 minutes pouring over the contents. Seems the political world even comes across in *USA Today's* truncated reporting format.

All of this is a long way of saying we really didn't dawdle over breakfast. At 6:35 we were out of IHOP and in search of an infant car seat. Seems hospitals these days won't let you leave the premises with a baby who is not securely stowed in an officially blessed and approved safety restraint system. (My father claims my brother and I were just placed on the backseat wrapped in a blanket…but I suspect we were probably at least curled in Mom's arms—even if she wasn't wearing a seatbelt…that mandatory procedure had yet to come into existence.) Not wanting to be stuck at the front door of the hospital, Melanie directed we procure the required accoutrement before heading to see our potential birth mother. This meant we pulled into the first logical candidate for such an item, K-Mart. If I thought early morning IHOP in Tucson offered interesting characters, the restaurant had nothing on the nearby K-Mart.

In addition to the standard crowd, this K-Mart offered cowboys in mud stained jeans, street urchins seeking easy plunder, and more than one apparent alcoholic attempting to walk off the booze by wandering the aisles in search of the mythical blue-light special. (I am dating myself…but I recall the glory days of walking into K-Mart and hearing announcements for the latest blue-light special, a sale distinguished by a flashing blue light attached to shopping cart.)

Melanie took one look at this crowd and immediately decided our time in K-Mart would be markedly shorter than the 30 minutes spent in IHOP. She made a dash for the child/baby wear section of the store, with me in tow pushing a rickety shopping cart. I always find Melanie's ability to make quick purchase decisions in "adverse" situations amusing. Normally, she is willing to take the time necessary to compare style, color and price. At moments like the one described above she is much less picky. With the quick declaration that "we will purchase a nicer seat when we get back home," Melanie directed I grab the nearest box and head for the registers. At least the trip back through the aisles offered one more opportunity for people watching. Guess you could say I am a bit of a social voyeur.

Melanie's haste in departing K-Mart meant we were headed for the hospital by 0700…still 60 minutes ahead of visiting hours, but Melanie was counting on my inevitable ability to get lost as a backup time killer. For once she was wrong about my male predilection for misdirection. Instead of circling the city in search Tucson General, I pulled into the parking lot without a collection of u-turns or unplanned gas station stops. Even more amazingly, I actually managed to read the signs that pointed to an obstetrics parking area—why didn't I think of looking for such obvious guidance the previous night? Strike two against my ability to navigate without an ever-observant co-driver.

Even at this early hour the parking lot was packed…full size pickup trucks cover a space and half, so maybe the sense of crowding reflected this favored choice of transportation rather than a teaming mass of humanity. In any case, the search for a suitable place to dump the car burned another 10 minutes. We were wear-

Adopting Ainsley

ing down the clock one small event at a time. But like all good things, even this excuse for delaying the inevitable was bound to come to an end. Eventually one of the super-sized pickups backed out and opened a slot big enough for our rental and two other subcompacts. I backed the Chevy in…best procedure for ensuring a quick getaway…and followed Melanie into the hospital. Given my wife's pace, our dawdling was now at an end—we were headed for the baby ward at high speed.

Security at the front door was even tighter than the gamut I had encountered a mere 10 hours earlier. Back to pulling out multiple forms of identification and placing my John Hancock on various pieces of paper that are probably still on file in some obscure office. All this resulted in my being handed a sticker that said "visitor" in bright blue letters and…helpfully…a map of the entire facility. At least today I would not be wandering aimlessly through the corridors hoping for a glimpse of some obviously pregnant woman wrapped in an uncomfortable gown.

Melanie required no such navigational aid. Blessed with an ability to read instructional signs adhered to the hospital walls— this must be a female capability men have been denied, all my buddies also claim to never see said postings—she resumed a rapid march toward our intended destination. This clip, however, belied a real anxiety about our situation. Before we arrived at obstetrics Melanie asked me at least three times what our "odds" might be and expressed concerns about a negative outcome in two sentences separated by less than 10 feet of the linoleum bedecked hallway. What do you say in such situations? I stuck with my optimist's approach to life and hoped for the best.

As had been the case at night, the doors leading into our chosen ward were sealed behind magnetic locks. Unlike the night before, there was actually someone standing by the door checking names and proffering official forms of identification. Apparently baby thieves are more like to strike in the daylight…kind of like our neighborhood back in DC…only in this case one certainly could not assume no one was home. The residents in this ward were all largely confined to their rooms—with husbands and boyfriends on the prowl in the hallways. Takes a pretty brazen or clever thief to operate in these conditions, and, yet, it was clear someone in the hospital administration was afraid a babynapping was just waiting to happen.

Despite the fact we were 30 minutes ahead of posted visiting time; the guard motioned us through the double doors and back into the hands of an ever-pleasant obstetrics staff. I didn't recognize anyone—unsurprising given my late night arrival and normal staff rotations—but Melanie quickly identified a few of the folks she had spoken with the previous day. A quick hello, a few inquires later, and we knew the young lady had slept well, the baby was fine and no one had come by to visit. On a more disturbing front, we learned the baby had spent the night with mom rather than heading to the nursery—a poor sign for potential adoptive parents, as this is an indication mom is bonding with the child—and the birth mother was still expressing ambivalence about her decision.

Melanie found this news extremely unsettling and immediately began hunting for Alfred's contact number and email address on her Blackberry. Our wayward attorney had not been in touch overnight—no shock with that development—and, as I tried to explain to Melanie, there was low to no probability he was going to be answering a phone at this time of day. My bet was that he was still sleeping off one-arm curls. I should have made the bet; Melanie had to settle with leaving a voice message and an email. Suffice it to say the tone and verbiage would likely stir a response sometime in the next 12 hours.

At 8 o'clock we knocked on the young lady's door. A nurse let us in to witness a smiling mother cooing to her new daughter. I could see Melanie's heart sink. Instead of just turning to leave—as logic should have dictated—we tried to break the ice with small

Adopting Ainsley

talk. What a waste of time. While small-talk comes naturally to me, particularly if it's about China, motorcycles, or women, the same could not be said of our potential birth mother. She managed a quiet "Good Morning" and acknowledged she was "doing well." This was going to be a long day.

I was spared further painful wracking of the brain by a knock on the door and a hearty greeting from the hospital social worker. I've now met with a fair number of people who serve in this capacity…they all come from a single mold. Frumpy, slightly overweight, and endlessly effervescent. If they had not opted for a career dealing with the confused, all of these ladies would have made great car salespersons. They can talk—about everything and nothing, and they make you feel like a close personal friend in less than five minutes of conversation. If anyone could get the young lady to communicate it was going to be the social worker. Melanie and I excused ourselves and headed for the waiting room.

Now I have been known to cuss and fuss about modernity. These snide comments are typically aimed at cell phones with too many options, televisions I cannot figure out how to turn on, and cars that no longer lend themselves to shade tree repairs. I am not, however, about to bad-mouth my ability to log on to the Internet from almost anywhere in America. I have dialed into the web while riding trains, sitting in traffic, and—don't tell anyone—aboard endless flights across the United States. About 2 minutes after walking into the waiting room I was on line, finally reading news of interest and catching up on email. I give Melanie grief about her Blackberry…but have to admit I would be lost without my laptop. Same addiction, mine just comes in a larger format.

The nice thing about the web and email is how much time one can waste conducting seemingly useful functions. I didn't even notice 45 minutes had elapsed before the social worker found us to pass along news. "She has not made up her mind." Great, not exactly what we were hoping for —a decision, either way, would have made life much less stressful at that moment. "She does want to speak with an attorney, and she would like me to come back this afternoon." Wonderful, now we were condemned to stewing for at least another 6-8 hours.

Having passed her message without violating any patient-social worker confidentiality agreement, our new best friend abruptly departed to continue her work day. I looked at Melanie, Melanie looked at me, and then she dialed Alfred's number for the 8th time that morning. (I was beginning to wonder how many messages his answering system could hold or when the angry tone of these missives would finally cause the machine to fry.) Surprise, surprise… this time an actual human actually answered the call. Melanie almost dropped her phone in shock.

I was only privy to one side of the conversation, but it was obvious Alfred was nowhere to be found. According to his secretary, the attorney in question was out with a client and she had no idea when he would be coming into the office. (A polite way of covering for a boss who clearly suffered significant timeliness issues.) Melanie made it clear we expected a call and some advice on how to proceed. "I'll pass the message along," was the best she could get from the secretary. Good thing the nurses didn't have a blood pressure cuff on my wife at that point…we would have been headed for the emergency room. I knew this as Melanie's face was now beat red and her voice had assumed a tone usually reserved for moments when I have really screwed up…like bleaching a full wash load of colored cloths.

"Have Alfred call me as soon as you contact him." As best I could tell the secretary responded to the affirmative and then hung up. Melanie stood up and declared this was "becoming very aggravating." Timing not being my strong point, I replied with a snarky "becoming?" and was rewarded with a look that wilts flowers and causes large dogs to scamper away with tail between the legs. "Look smart ass, it would be nice to get some answers." I agreed in an emphatic matter and went back to shopping the web. At moments like this I have learned silence is the best means of ensuring I will survive until tomorrow.

Melanie strode off to see if she could get further information from the social worker. I went back to the email and researching my latest project. No sense in two of us wandering the corridors. If nothing else I was available to answer any bidding from the young lady. Needless to say, none was forthcoming. So I returned to writing, another hobby that can fill endless hours. If you don't like to be seen talking to yourself in public; take up writing. You can have the same dialogue without appearing loony. Quite the contrary, people will actually be deluded into believing you are either very productive or an intellectual. Whatever you do, don't actually admit to being an author…once that news creeps out you're apt to be dismissed as unemployed or lazy. Trust me; everyone knows 99 percent of all self-proclaimed authors don't make a dime at their chosen profession. This one included.

Chapter VII
Disappointment Realized

Apparently there is nothing that cannot happen.
—Mark Twain

I pounded on the keyboards for about 20 minutes before Melanie returned to find me. Seems she finally spoke with Alfred and had learned a few things. First, despite Alfred's promise all potential birth mothers spent time talking to his on-call psychologist, this young lady had not gone through the screening process. Second, Alfred felt it would be a good idea to have a local attorney working on our behalf and had contacted one of his collaborators in Tucson. The gentleman in question was supposed to arrive within the hour. And, finally, Alfred bid we "hang in" as one never knows how this type of situation might evolve. None of this was music to Melanie's ears, but at least she felt we finally had an "expert" coming to our assistance.

Having passed along the news, Melanie suggested we once again try to communicate with the new mother...and I thought I was the optimist in the family. We walked down the hall to discover a closed door. "Doctor's examine," was the best explanation the staff would offer. We decided to stand by. Who knows, maybe the doctor would prompt some introspection that worked in our favor. Fifteen minutes later the door swung open, the doc looked at us, and went on with his rounds without speaking a word. Sigh, about now I was willing to kill for a break in patient-doctor confidentiality.

Before I had time to do more than momentarily contemplate my options on this front a slightly disheveled figure bearing an attorney-type brief case strode past us and into the young lady's room. Once again the door swung shut, and we were left to ponder our navels in the hallway. I have an "inny"...not much to think about there. So I shuffled my feet and pretended to not be interested in the crowd that was wandering past. Maternity wards in public hospitals—to be polite—have quite the cross-section for clientele.

In addition to the working middle class whose insurance affords no other option, we were witness to obvious gang-bangers, very young teen moms (they are the ones with mothers my age standing guard), and the destitute of America. Everyone, it seemed, but us, was capable of having children. The parade was doing nothing for Melanie's morale...I was simply trying to absorb all the skin art. Tucson apparently has quite the thriving tattoo trade. I watched everything from tribal to obvious gang symbols pass along the corridors—and that was just on the women. The male occupants of the hallway were equally adorned, but usually with larger artwork. Made me wonder about getting another tattoo to add to the collection. Melanie clearly was reading my mind; I could hear the word "no" without her even bothering to verbalize the thought.

Twenty minutes after the apparent lawyer disappeared into the birth mother's room, the door swung open. Out walked the disheveled character, briefcase firmly in hand. With a passing glance in our direction, the gentleman began heading for the exit. "Excuse me," I finally declared, "who are you?" "Oh, I'm here to represent a couple considering adoption." I was floored. "In other words," I finally seethed, "you are here to work for us." Pause. You could see the wheels turning in this guy's head...on some very rusty tracks. "Oh, you must be Eric Anderson and Melanie Sloan." The words "no shit" crossed my mind; fortunately something more polite came out of my mouth. "Yes, and we would like to know the status of this potential adoption."

The best the attorney could offer was that the young lady had yet to make up her mind, but promised to do so before the end of the day. Now I was pissed. This clown had walked past us without asking who we were and then had proceeded to question the potential birth mother without even asking for our insights or concerns. That was not going to happen again, ever. Struggling to keep my anger in check, I reminded the erstwhile attorney that he in fact worked for *us,* and that he would have no more contact with the young lady without actually speaking to us first. "Is that clear?" I found myself asking, rhetorically. (I figured this bozo could be replaced almost immediately. There is no shortage of attorneys anywhere in America.) "Yes," was all he would offer. With that he handed Melanie a business card and walked out the door. My opinion of Alfred had now hit rock bottom.

Time to take matters back into our own hands. Melanie knocked on the young lady's door and asked if we could come in. "Yes." Most I had heard from this quarter all day. Melanie then quietly and politely explained we were standing by for a decision—and that we would understand regardless of the choice the birth mother made. This drew much head nodding, but little else. Finally, the young lady declared she would make a decision before 5pm and tell us at that point. Melanie agreed that was fine and indicated I should climb out of the less-than-comfortable chair reserved for visitors. "Let's get lunch," she directed.

The last five-and-half hours of sitting in hospital air conditioning poorly prepared us for Tucson in August. Hot was an understatement. Damn hot would be more appropriate. Have I previously mentioned GM's failure to provide adequate air conditioning for the Cobalt? At the risk of being verbose allow me to repeat that observation here. Even with the air turned all the way up and the windows rolled down that yellow car was a furnace. All we needed to make s'mores were a few graham crackers, a chocolate bar and marshmallows. Squish same together and leave on backseat…two minutes later dessert would be ready for service.

Even Melanie, who is notorious for being cold in any environment, found this intolerable. "We need a lunch place, now." In the best of all possible worlds such an order would have caused me to pull into the nearest bar offering a burger and beer. This was not the best of all possible worlds. We were highly unlikely to impress our potential birth mother if I returned from lunch reeking of Budweiser. (My wife is the food and wine snob—I'm willing to consume almost anything…including the American beer that caused Asians to open their own breweries.) So I opted for a local version of TGIF and pulled into the parking lot.

By the time we made the front door of the restaurant it was clear our current attire was going to create problems. Not because we were under or over dressed, but because the sweat running down our backs was going to freeze as soon as we slid into the vinyl booths. Too late for a quick change or a run back to the apartment. Committed to finding something for lunch in the closest proximity to the hospital, we agreed to take a seat by the large picture windows. If nothing else the radiant sunlight would help take the chill out of a restaurant that was cooled to at least 65 degrees—perhaps colder. I've traveled all over the planet and only Americans seem to think 65 is a comfortable temperature for air conditioning. One wouldn't "heat" to 65, why do we think air conditioning requires such extremes?

Enough whining, back to the story at hand. After glancing through the menu we both agreed salads and ice tea seemed like logical choices. We also agreed this was a good place to discuss what was to come upon our return to the hospital. I voted for an adoption—after all, who would give up a full ride to medical school in exchange for raising a baby? Melanie was more pessimistic. "She's keeping the baby." Melanie was not mincing words. "Why do you think so?" I was trying to keep the conversation upbeat.

"Because she's taking so long to reach a decision—and it's clear the two of them are bonding." Melanie was now reciting the adoptive parents' worst case scenario to me. She was right. All of our reading, and even Alfred, had warned that a mother who has a hard time deciding on the wisdom of adoption is unlikely to go through with the option, particularly when she has come to the adoption option very late in the pregnancy. I wasn't ready to surrender that easily. "She still hasn't contacted her parents; maybe they will offer a dose of common sense." "Don't hold your breath," Melanie really was on the downside of positive.

Lunch came and went on largely untouched plates. Ever notice how you lose your appetite when the world throws a lot of stress in your direction. This is nature's way of protecting you from a violent disbursement of the latest meal upon encountering even more turbulence. This reaction served the caveman well when he or she had to run for their life…in the modern world it just prevents unsightly accidents. We waved off the prospect of dessert and began steeling ourselves for a return to the hospital. The clock now read 1:30, at worst we only had three and a half hours to go. I should have argued for the beer.

Finding parking on our return to the hospital was no easier than it had been in the morning. More large trucks baking in the sun. This absence of adequate parking spaces at medical facilities has always left me wondering…how we are supposed to transport the sick and ailing to a doctor? Walking is typically out, and public transportation in most American cities is best described as a band aid on a gushing wound. Come on guys; factor in parking when designing the next hospital.

After two rotations of the lot a space finally opened near a back entrance. I wedged the Cobalt between two jacked-up Ford 150s and joined Melanie in a languid march back to the obstetrics ward. The uncertainly, coupled with signs we were headed for a significant disappointment, simply drained the energy from my body. The mind was willing, the legs were not so cooperative—but on we trudged.

The guard at the baby ward's front doors waved us through like we were long-standing customers. I suspect he had seen a lot of Melanie during her pacing of the corridors. I slinked toward the waiting room, hoping for a diversion in the form of email and a few more lines of scribble on my project. Melanie headed back toward the young lady's room, likely in search of a decision. This was rapidly becoming a spirit-crushing event.

I was a tad surprised when Melanie returned in less than two minutes. "She's made a decision and would like to speak with both of us." I closed the computer and grabbed my crap. One way or another we were going to be freed from more time in these sticky seats. "Did she indicate her intentions?" My feeble effort at preparing the mind for potential bad news. "Nope." This is Melanie's standard response when she is in no mood for my chitchat and is tired of waiting for me to get on the move. I shoved the computer into its briefcase and stuffed my papers in a folder. Melanie was already headed for the door.

I knew things were going south the minute we entered the birth mother's room. Mom and baby were curled up together on the bed. In place of the stressed out young lady I had witnessed over the last 18 hours, there was now a sense of calm. Over the years I've discovered this is a common phenomenon. Upon reaching a decision on a major concern—for better or worse—many people exude a palpable sense of relief. This aurora tends to fill the space around them, in a sense serving to calm those who had also been exposed to the previous mental storm. We partook of the karma by choosing to sit at the foot of her bed and soak in the scene.

"I have spoken with my parents." Ah ha, as Melanie had suspected, Mom and Dad were really not unreachable, they were simply not informed. "They have agreed to help me with the baby and to care for her while I attend medical school." I felt like someone had jabbed me in the gut with the blunt end of a pool cue. (Been there, done that, it hurts…trust me.) "I really appreciate your traveling all this way, and you will make great parents."

Melanie had a look of complete disbelief on her face. Despite having accurately assessed the situation from the onset, she was not ready to surrender without an application of logic. "You do understand how difficult it will be to raise a child and attend school?" "Yes," came the reply, "but my Mom has agreed to move in with me to help while I am in class." That response did little to sooth Melanie's sense of disbelief. "Your mother is going to leave her husband to live with you for the next six years?" "Yes, that's what she told me." Melanie refrained from what would normally have been her next sarcastic observation—are you out of your mind?

For a moment I thought we were done. Melanie had other ideas. "I know we can't change your mind and certainly do not want to take away your child, but have you completely considered the enormity and consequence of this decision." This caused a slight pause from the interlocutor lying in the hospital bed. "I have. I realize that I am committed to at least another seven years of school and this may be my only chance to have a child." I literally had to turn away in order to mask my incongruity. Here was an 18 year-old telling me she would be too old for more children at age 26. Guess she had forgotten who she was talking to. My son was born when I was 36 and my ex was 33. And we were far from the oldest people in the delivery room that day. Such logic coming from a biology major who intended to be a medical doctor entirely defied even my knuckle-dragger's sense of logic. But what do I know?

Melanie, on the other hand, immediately realized we were now dealing with the delusional. "People have children well into their 30s; a decision often made as a result of wanting to complete an education and begin a career that makes responsibly raising a child possible." This drew no response. The young lady had made up her mind—and we were now just an uncomfortable reminder of her foolish decision to avoid telling Mom and Dad from the outset. I nudged Melanie. "It's time to go, dear." Melanie gave me a resigned glance and stood up. I grabbed my briefcase and joined her.

"Take care, we wish you all the best." A feeble "Thank you" came from the bed. We headed for the exit in a rapid dash. I'm still not sure if the most appropriate description of our condition was hurt or humiliated. Probably a mixture of the two. We had just traveled across the country at the drop of a hat. Spent an extra $500 to expedite the home study. And were now faced with the prospect of going home with greatly diminished expectations. All so that an emotionally unstable 18 year-old could make a decision she should have considered about 8 months earlier.

In all fairness, Alfred had warned us this type of thing could happen. We had also spoken with other couples who had been party to multiple disappointing situations, but one always likes to think, "This won't happen to me." Wrong again. Cars are stolen, jobs are lost, and pets die. There is nothing you can do except stand up, dust off the damage, and start over again.

We went back to the apartment and packed. After briefly considering the option of staying for a few more days—Tucson is said to have a few great golf courses—we opted to find the first flight out in the morning. I drove back to the K-Mart and returned the car seat. Different crowd, same ambiance. Melanie found a restaurant in the foothills overlooking the city and we retreated to a dark table for a glass of wine and decent meal. Tomorrow was a whole new day, and Alfred promised there would be more opportunities. Back to waiting.

Chapter VIII
Back to the Paperwork

The government of my country snubs honest simplicity, but fondles artistic villainy, and I think I might have developed into a very capable pickpocket if I had remained in the public service a year or two.

—*Mark Twain*

If natural procreation required all the paperwork necessary for adoption there would be no need for birth control…government would have accomplished the feat without medical intervention. While our experience in Tucson was certainly disappointing, the outcome was a bit of a blessing. You may recall that before my mad dash to parts unknown—you can see them from Tucson—I made a stop at the Conjoined Foundation to begin our formal home study. In theory, one cannot take an adoptive child across state lines, or to one's domicile, without having competed one of these bureaucratic exercises in futility.

I use the word "theory" here purposefully. Unless you are engaged in an international adoption that requires legally reentering the United States, no one is going to ask you for documentation when boarding an aircraft with an infant in your arms. Instead, the rational airline crew will presume the child is yours, because only the insane want to actually fly with a baby. If the crying doesn't drive you nuts, the dizzying array of equipment necessary to sustain a small child will serve to deter all but the most determined erstwhile parent. (I know of what I speak. Having now flown with Ainsley on a number of occasions, I am fond of arguing I could use a Sherpa to help with the mountain of associated accoutrements. My sister-in-law, who has been to Nepal, likes to remind me what I really need is a porter—as no Sherpa worthy of the title actually totes gear. My response to this cultural snobbery…"Sherpa, porter, doesn't matter, just give me someone capable of hauling some of the stuff.")

I have pointed this lack of concern about documents out to Melanie on a number of occasions. She remains unimpressed with my logic. As far as Melanie is concerned, if the law requires a home study be complete before we cross state lines with a child, then we will have a home study. Did I already mention she also promptly pays parking tickets and typically adheres to the speed limit? I should have known my scoff-law approach to dealing with seemingly mindless government mandates was not going to carry the day in our house.

What all this really means is that we could have been parked in Tucson for an extended period of time. You see, simply starting the home study by writing a check and answering a few harmless questions was not going to accomplish the mission. Diane remained adamant about interviewing Melanie in person…and then there was the whole pesky house inspection. So, even if things had gone smoothly in Tucson, I would have been sitting in Arizona with a very small child while my wife flew back to Washington to facilitate completion of this "critical" document.

Given the apparent life-or-death nature of this document, I began to wonder where the damn thing actually went. What body of experts would pour over the details of our lives to ensure we were worthy of raising a child? I had visions of bespectacled, bearded psychologists and psychiatrists critically evaluating every word Diane placed on the pages. At the very least, I thought the home study would land in the hands of attorneys and law enforcement types. You know, the three-piece suit crowd and large men wearing mirrored sun glasses and Smokey-the-Bear hats. Boy was I delusional.

Adopting Ainsley

The home study is actually dictated by the Interstate Compact on the Placement of Children (ICPC). Enacted in all 50 states, the District of Columbia and Virgin Islands, the ICPC was originally intended to facilitate adoptions across state lines by assuring the suitability of the adoptive families. As a result of our convoluted legal system, local officials face significant jurisdictional issues when trying to ensure proper care for children who are adopted or placed in foster care in another state. To help alleviate these concerns, the ICPC dictates a "sending agency" follow certain procedural requirements when requesting permission of a "receiving state" prior to the interstate placement of a child.

To accomplish this agenda, the ICPC outlines four key objectives: determination of the suitability of the interstate placement; determination of any circumstances bearing on the protection of the child; obtaining complete information on which to "evaluate a projected placement before it is made;" and promoting "appropriate jurisdictional arrangements for the care of the children placed." In other words, the ICPC is supposed to be looking out for the welfare of the child and society as a whole. It should prevent states from shifting support burdens to other jurisdictions and ensure that adoptive parents are suited for their new loved one. Unarguably, a worthy agenda.

Now here's the problem. The ICPC review process is not entrusted to a star chamber. Nor is it guaranteed to be smooth or timely. More than one couple has complained the ICPC review took 10-15 business days, while other would-be parents have observed the entire process seemed to occur in mere hours. It all depends on where you adopt and who is completing the document review. A case in point, when the Virginia Department of Social Services conducted a ICPC programmatic review a couple of years back the inspectors found a lack of uniform staff training "leads to un-standardized interpretation/understanding of information." Hmmm, not a warm fuzzy when sitting in some god-forsaken hotel room with a screaming child.

Eric C Anderson

What I'm trying to say, is that a dig through materials associated with the day-to-day conduct of the ICPC reveals a process essentially administered by mid-ranking state officials assigned to the various agencies charged with family services. I am certain many of these officials have honorable intentions and seek to serve to the best of their ability. Trained, licensed psychologists or psychiatrists, however, they largely are not. My suspicion is that the ICPC process is overwhelmingly conducted by people who majored in education or sociology. But, as we shall see momentarily, certainly not English.

So what does a home study report look like—what does one get for $1,900, fingerprinting and a local police records evaluation? Well, I could bore you with a redacted copy of the whole report. (Melanie insists people should not know everything about us…I'm less reluctant…but if I ever want to engage in bedroom gymnastics again, uh, you would get the blacked-out version.) I'm not that mean. Plus, a lot of the document is just plain boring. But allow me to amuse you with a few gems. Keep in mind, this is what determines if we actually get to adopt.

Here's how Diane's masterpiece introduces the potential father—in other words, me:

> *"Mr Anderson is an attractive Caucasian male with blue eyes, strawberry blond hair, and a fair complexion. He is 5'8" and weights (sic) 145 pounds. He presents in a direct and articulate manner. Mr Anderson describes himself as responsible, intelligent, active and logical."*

Right. The last time anyone described me as "attractive" was second grade. It's true, I have strawberry blond hair—at least that's the color of the hair which has not turned gray. I am 5'8" tall… but that diminishes with gravity and age on a daily basis. I have been known to "present" in a "direct and articulate manner"…my friends and Melanie describe this as "blunt" and "verbose"…needless to say, I like Diane's description better. And the last sentence?

Adopting Ainsley

Hey, brag when you get the chance, who knows what the social worker is going to say elsewhere in the report.

It gets better. Try this section on "emotional stability and maturity."

> "During the home study the social worker asked Mr Anderson...if [he] had a history of criminal activity, domestic violence, substance abuse, or sexual abuse in [his] family background or personal history. Mr Anderson states he does not have a history of criminal activity, child abuse, sexual abuse, substance abuse, or domestic violence."

Of course I'm going to say that. What kind of idiot would reply to any of those questions to the affirmative and still believe they were going to be allowed to adopt? As for the family background, trust me, no one called my parents or siblings to see if they had issues in the above areas. Again, this report is not being read by people wearing police uniforms...it's a document for other social workers. Verifying the veracity of the subjects is apparently not a major concern.

Ok, ok, I'll get off my soapbox and move along. Here's how Diane summarized our "discipline and parenting abilities." (I like the pairing on this title—think about it, "discipline abilities"... sounds like a resume section for someone applying to work in an entirely different adult occupation...if you know what I mean.)

> "Mr Anderson and Ms Sloan agree on basic child rearing philosophies and they will share in parenting responsibilities. They intend to support each other's parenting decisions. They will discuss any differences they may have in private away from their child. They intend to encourage and support their children, and will provide ongoing opportunities for their children to explore their interests and skills. They will establish a daily routine and a structured home. When appropriate, they will be flexible. They will raise their children with love and acceptance. As parents they will attempt to be reasonable in their expectations for their children."

Whoa. At this point the average parent reading this text is either gagging or chuckling. The ones who are gagging hit on the agreement to discuss any differences in private…right. I grew up with two educators, we knew when they had "differences"…even in private. I'd bet most of you can make a similar observation. The gaggers are also probably choking on the "flexible" line. Trust me, Melanie has yet to define what that means…other than "flexible" translates as "do as I tell you." I'm thinking "flexible" means, "do what you want, so long as I don't get in trouble with your mother."

The parents who are chuckling, on the other hand, likely started rolling their eyes on the "daily routine and structured home" line. Daily routine…hmmm…does that mean get out of bed, eat breakfast, go to school, do homework, eat dinner, go to bed? Or does that mean a household with a purposeful design intended to facilitate intellectual development? The realists (count me in) naturally point to the former. I'm sure Diane thought it was the later. Oh, the chuckling does not end there. What's this whole line about "attempt to be reasonable in their expectations?" I guarantee you, I'm "reasonable." Ainsley will get top marks, be an outstanding athlete, and be a sweet teenager. Melanie is equally "reasonable," she has selected either Harvard or Yale as likely schools for Ainsley's bachelor's degree.

Now on to the pesky discipline issue. Here's Diane's description of our plans for keeping the occasionally unruly child firmly in hand.

> *"Mr. Anderson and Ms Sloan do not believe in corporal punishment or harsh discipline. When discipline is necessary, they will use time out, redirect behavior, or deny a privilege. They will teach their children there are consequences for their behaviors. They will encourage their children to take responsibility for their behavior and decisions."*

Trust me, my parents did not take such an idealistic approach. My mother yielded a wicked wooden spoon and my father was known to occasionally spank…after he gave up on that whole

Adopting Ainsley

"speak wisdom to the child" silliness. Apparently, Melanie and I have seen the light and joined the whole new age child-rearing movement. I, for one, however, am going to stand back and let Melanie discuss behavioral consequences with a rampaging three year-old. Better yet, I think I'll go to the gym and let Melanie discuss behavioral consequences with the three year-old. All I have to say is, dent my motorcycle and plan on losing a lot of privileges... like, oh say, leaving your room for the next month.

This bad combination of pulp fiction and popular psychology goes on for a sum total of seven pages. And culminates with the following "agency evaluation."

> *"Mr Anderson and Ms Sloan's decision to adopt reflects a mutual decision to be loving and supportive parents. They have a strong marriage. They are enthusiastically supported in their desire to adopt by their extended families and close friends. Mr Anderson and Ms Sloan will provide a loving and stable home for their children and are approved for the adoption of a child age one or under, of either gender, and of any race."*

Yawn. That's the best Diane could do? After opening with that description of me as "attractive," I was expecting flowery language that suggested we were fit for sainthood and should be allowed to adopt a whole school if so desired. Guess I should be more appreciative. Diane thoughtfully left off the tattoos and the whole traumatized receptionist bit. She also did not mention the basement filled with tools that could remove little fingers faster than I can yell "don't touch that."

But now that I think about it...all it would have taken is a slip of the pen, or in this case the keyboard, and all our hopes would be for naught. You see, someone in a basement office at an unknown state capitol might read between the spaces and discover I actually like cold beer or unstructured events and thereby deem us unworthy of raising another human being. Cats, dogs...fine...but a child and all the associated disarray...that's right out. Daunting proposition if you think about it. I, as usual did not. Melanie, of course, spent hours fretting the hidden messages in Diane's workmanship.

You know what I really think? I strongly suspect the private agencies that specialize in crafting home studies have lists of accepted syntax that may be pieced together to assemble a finished document. Replace "client's name here" with "Eric" or "Melanie" and the whole thing is done in 60 minutes. Oh, I guess that's not fair. Diane did actually talk to us and did visit the house. That would put my time estimate for the product at somewhere around 4 hours. Given Diane's original bill for $1,900 that converts to more than 450 bucks an hour. I know attorneys who don't make that much over a 60 minute period. Damn good living…perhaps I'm in the wrong business.

"Hey Dear, do we still know about job opportunities at a home studies office?"

Chapter IX
Back to L.A.

Yes, even I am dishonest. Not in many ways, but in some. Forty-one, I think it is.

—Mark Twain

Waiting is a pathetic game. I have never been good at this peculiar sport. As one of my more blunt friends would put it, "patience my ass, I'm going out to kill something, now!" Melanie, as you might guess, is little better. She has figured out all the routes to the local gym that don't include stoplights…all so that she can avoid waiting the extra 30 seconds. You can imagine the stewing that was taking place behind our front door.

This sense of unrealized anticipation was further aggravated by the fact our little Tucson adventure had completely derailed Melanie's plans to escape Washington during the dog days of summer. Rather than enjoying a vacation—Melanie likes to flee the District when Congress is not in session—we were compelled to sit in the house staring at the phone. A phone that simply did not ring. Oh, we contemplated moving this endeavor to the back deck, but August in Washington is best understood by spending 15 minutes in a steam room…wearing your mother's heaviest fur coat. In other words, it's hot, sticky, and otherwise, just plain damn uncomfortable.

In this kind of weather, even the motorcycle generates little enthusiasm. The prospect of sitting in traffic with a motor emitting endless heat immediately between one's legs even causes me to think twice. (That, and the very strange looks I get when riding dressed in a seersucker suit. Apparently, this is a gross violation of the Harley riders' code of conduct.) If the heat and humidity are not a sufficient deterrent, there is always the prospect of unforeseen thunderstorms. Melanie and I have an agreement. No riding in the rain or snow. The latter needs little explanation, the former is just Melanie worrying. But rather than risk yet another round of questions concerning my commonsense, I shy away from the bike when the weatherman predicts showers. Yup, August in Washington just plain sucks.

So August comes and goes with no further word from Alfred. Melanie began to suspect this extended silence could be directly linked to a scathing conversation we held with the wayward attorney upon our return from Tucson. Rather than risk another round of such tomfoolery, we chose to provide Alfred with very specific guidance. Speaking very slowly and employing no verbiage with more than three syllables, Melanie and I informed Alfred that we would not be dashing off to see young ladies who had not completed his initial acceptance screening. Alfred stammered, declared all situations were unique, and then agreed to our terms. Sometimes I wondered who was working for whom…but Alfred was still our man.

So August comes and goes. September opened with little more promise. Congress came back to town and the kiddies went to school. All of which brought traffic to a snarled halt. Washington DC is a commuter's nightmare without school buses and soccer moms. Throw those ingredients in to the mix and you have a real witches brew. I returned to traveling by riding the dashed white lines…and hoping no one chose to switch lanes before I was able to grab the brakes and issue a finely honed selection of epitaphs. My mother would definitely not be proud of what driving in DC has done for my vocabulary.

By mid-September Melanie was ready to set Alfred on fire. I suggested thinking about another lawyer; only to be brutally reminded we had placed a significant wad of cash in the lax attorney's wallet. Sigh. These are the times that try a man's soul. Attempt to console your wife and you get an ass chewing. Seek to offer alternative solutions…and you get an ass chewing. Do nothing…you guessed…and you get an ass chewing. I decided it was time for me to get busy in the wood shop. Melanie is not enamored of the basement or my sawdust—that makes my shop an ideal locale when things are not going as planned on the first or second floor of the house.

All of which brings us to early October. While the November elections are keeping Melanie busy…the politicos like to leak dirt during any campaign, but are particularly vicious when the White House is up for grabs…she still has time to worry the lack of news from California. I know this is the case, as I am reminded of Alfred's silence on a daily basis. Furthermore, Melanie is starting to openly wonder if we shouldn't have gone with the Ethiopian option after all. Having learned my lesson, I offer a sympathetic ear and keep my trap shut. There is nothing useful my 80IQ is going to add to this conversation.

And then it happens…the phone rings and Alfred's number appears on the caller ID. Ok, so I've let the cat out the bag. Yes, I screen phone calls. Like any other red-blooded American male, there are times when I just don't want to speak with the family, inlaws, or telemarketers. Melanie claims this is the case most of the time. She may have me on this one. I am known to turn off my cell and "forget" to power the infernal object back up for days. Similarly, I have developed a clear allergy to answering the house phone. If it's important they'll call back…or contact Melanie. Works for me, until Melanie wearies of this little Luddite act, then I'm back to grabbing calls on this first ring. Better to suffer some idiot on the far end of the line than get repeat lectured for ignoring the phone.

Where was I? Oh, yes, Alfred is on the line…with news of a prospective birth mother! Melanie grabs the phone from my hand

and dispatches me to fetch a handset from elsewhere in the house. I told you patience is not her strong suit. Back to Alfred. Seems Alfred has been in contact with a young woman from Bakersfield who is now seven months pregnant and looking for adoptive parents. She is healthy, has completed all his intake paperwork, and is going to be in LA the following day. All Alfred wants to know from us is can we be there as well?

He should have known it was not going to be that easy. Melanie is already firing away with questions. "How old is she?" "Sixteen." Pause. "Did you say sixteen?" Alfred answers to the affirmative. "Drug use?" "None that she's admitting." "Alcohol use?" This one causes Alfred to carefully select his words. "Twice." Melanie looks at me and blinks. "Twice? How can you be that certain?" Alfred handles this better than I expected. "According to the young lady she went to parties two weekends in a row, got drunk, and had unprotected sex…hence the baby." He did warn us the majority of his mothers were not Brigham Young University students…seems he wasn't kidding.

Melanie lets this one go and moves on with the interrogation. "Father in the picture?" Alfred has this one in hand as well. "She says she did not know the father…there were two different males involved in the incidents." (I was a promiscuous high school student, but this is ridiculous…or maybe I'm suffering a bit of historic jealousy…I mean, there really was no surplus of girls throwing themselves at me…or any other male I knew at the time. Suffice it to say I suspect there is more to this story, but it's not my place to ask. That said, we shall revisit this whole father thing shortly.) At this point we are starting to think we have a trip to LA on our hands, so Melanie asks her final question.

"What is her race?" For the first time in memory, Alfred manages to stump both of us. "Indo-Fijian." "What?" (This is Melanie's reaction, I figured I must have misheard or Alfred has started happy hour early.) Our attorney tries again. "Fijian-Indian." So now

Adopting Ainsley

I'm scratching my head. Fijian-Indian? I've been a student of East Asia for the last 20 years and have not encountered this nationality. Well, I should be more honest. I have been a student of Northeast Asia for the last 20 years. The closest I have came to monitoring events in the south Pacific only happened during trips to Bali and the Philippines. In both cases the adventures required far more time at beaches and bars than actually reading the news...so it's possible I may have missed a few things. There goes my "know it all" reputation.

As it turns out, Indo-Fijians have an interesting history. They are descendents of Indians who British colonialists brought to Fiji as indentured servants between 1879 and 1916. While they found life on Fiji's sugar cane plantations less than delightful, many of these indentured servants chose to remain on the island after their five years of service had been completed. (Wise choice...given the option of returning to poverty in India or living on an island in paradise...well, I would have stayed in Fiji...you know what I mean?) In any case, Indo-Fijians now account for roughly 40 percent of the island's population, but have been leaving Fiji in droves—primarily to find better living conditions and escape a ridiculous political situation. (In the last 30 years the place has suffered 2 mutinies, 3 coups, and at least 4 constitutions...all this from a population of just over 800,000 people. Why aren't they at the beach instead of engaging in politics. Sunbathing is a hell of a lot more productive than squabbling over who gets to monitor coconut production.)

Without knowing any of this, Melanie asks what must have seemed like a natural next question. "What is her religion?" To say the least, I'm a little surprised at her change in direction—maybe she's worried the mom to be is a cannibal? (Melanie is self-admittedly no student of anything Asia. She occasionally will indulge my penchant for Korean food and suffers through sushi about once a year...but that's as far as she gets...you can forget chop sticks and all that other foreign stuff.) Alfred actually is ready for this. "She's Hindu." "Oh." And with that Melanie has no more questions.

Seeing an opportunity to get off the phone and away from our barrage of questions, Alfred fires back with his own. "So, are you flying out?" Melanie and I look at each other, nod yes, and with that we commit to another trip to LA. Alfred makes his last stab at covering his keister—"no guarantees, she may not like you." And with that hangs up knowing we will email a flight itinerary as soon as Melanie can blast through the options on expedia.com.

Melanie is a whiz with these on-line travel sites. I have watched her breeze through a hundred flight options, select a rental car, and make hotel reservations all in the course of about 15 minutes. Furthermore, she seems to have a knack for making frequent-flyer miles work…despite the airlines' concerted effort to make such an option almost impossible. In fact, I've seen her actually wrangle free baggage checks—no mean feat in a day when the airlines would like to charge us for actually carrying bags on board. (All of which begs the question, how does one get desired personal attire to the end destination? Mail it? Wear it? Purchase cheap stuff upon arrival?)

It turns out she is going to need all her talents tonight. There just did not seem to be a good way to get to LA in time for a ten o'clock meeting the next day. Or at least, I should say I did not see a reasonable option. Melanie was insistent we would be able to pull this off—non-stop—flying out of Reagan National. Believe it or not, there is a single daily non-stop flight from Hollywood for the Ugly to that actual McCoy on the West Coast. It's typically packed with people who refer to the Midwest as the "flyover zone" and believe there is no decent cuisine outside of a thin band between New York and Washington DC or Los Angeles and San Francisco. Normally attired in designer brands, these folks do not want to be troubled with trips to Baltimore or Dulles. They want their limos to make a short trip and thus arrive at the airport unmussed…the coffee still warm in its china cup.

Adopting Ainsley

And so we booked seats on the "beautiful people express." I tossed a decent shirt and gym clothes in a carry-on and then went in search of a plastic bad to tote my onboard snack and reading materials. Have I mentioned this perfect mode of transporting disposable consumables aboard an airline? By using a plastic bag I am spared lugging a briefcase and can walk off the plane relatively unburdened. The plastic bag simply goes in the trash with the newspapers, pulp fiction, and empty pretzel container. Melanie, you have properly surmised, is absolutely mortified by this habit. In her world one simply never shows up at an airport with goods stowed in old grocery bags…or worse yet, plastic sacks from cheap liquor stores. Such actions do not bespeak class…they scream mobile home park. Perhaps that's why she seems to frequently get in different security lines that I do. It may also explain why she will board separately from her husband. Or it could be my baseball cap that is on backwards, the paint-stained fleece, worn pair of shorts, and a tendency to wear clogs without socks.

I digress. By 10:30 we had accumulated everything required for a quick dash to the Left Coast and even managed to find clothing items that would make me appear suitable for fatherhood. Or at least appear respectable in the eyes of a 16-year old who was searching for responsible parents to raise her child. Melanie had also succeeded in rounding up a collection of reading material and had forbid me from dragging along a pile of folders with research material. Instead, I was handed the latest novel from her side of the bed and was told I should engage in some "good reading." This may surprise a few people. But I have little interest in fiction. There are simply too many good books on Asia, economics, and history to be wasting time on fiction. My wife, the English major, would beg to differ…perhaps that why she refers to me as a literary philistine. Or maybe that's just me bragging.

The real trick at this point was getting to sleep. Melanie typically resorts to sleeping pills. I have been known to use the stack of magazines on my side of the bed as a sleep aid, but tonight that was not going to do the trick. Besides, the latest version of *Rolling Stone* had a couple of good interviews and the motorcycle magazines had me thinking about road trip possibilities. Nope, I was going to have to break down and hope for better living through pharmaceuticals. "Uh, dear, can I have a sleeping pill?" Melanie gave me that knowing smile and popped open the bottle. "I was wondering when you would surrender." Sigh, why do women always have to be right?

The alarm went off at o'dark thirty as planned. Knowing I was going to spend a vast majority of the day sitting in a plane or dark conference room, the gym was a must. Melanie, as usual, opted for another thirty minutes of sleep. I can get Melanie to hit the gym three times a week…and she grumbles about every minute spent in the building. I, on the other hand, am on a first-name basis with most of the staff and refer to the place as my second home. The real challenge for me was shrugging off the mental shroud induced by Melanie's sleep aides. Sometimes coffee works, and then there are the days it takes dropping a 25lb dumbbell on my foot. Today it was clearly going to be the latter. I really need to get steel-toed gym shoes; the black toenails are simply unappealing.

I returned from the gym to find Melanie pacing behind the front door. "What took you so long?" Standard question…even when I am right on schedule. My lame defense, "I'm on time… and the plane is not slated to take off for another three hours." I should have known better than to offer any response. Melanie glared at me…and I ran for the shower. Sometimes cowardice is the wisest course of action. (My friend, the psychologist, refers to this as "fight or flight." I like to remind him the "fight" part worked for cavemen. Modern men have no recourse but "flight." He only agrees to this observation in private. In public situations he contends both options remain available. Typical psycho babble…no man has visibly sided with this observation…at least not in front of their wife.)

Adopting Ainsley

We arrive at Reagan National two hours before our flight. E-tickets firmly in hand...Melanie never goes to a check-in counter...that would entail more waiting...we head directly for security. Melanie promptly ditches her inappropriately attired husband and breezes through the process. I get subjected to the normal pat down and questions. Profiling is alive and well with the Transportation Security Administration. I'm not sure what suspect group I fall within, but clearly am considered unworthy of flying without strict screening and supervision.

Once clear of the "hats with sticks" we go off in search of Melanie's MacDonald's breakfast. And promptly encounter Melanie's primary complaint with National Airport, no Micky D's. Oh, there's a collection of the typical bad airport food options. These include sugar bomb cinnamon buns and very greasy eggs—who eats this stuff before flying?...the first option causes diabetic shock, the second induces multiple trips to the restroom—but no MacDonald's. Melanie had to make do with a Five Guys' sausage sandwich and a giant ice tea. I slurped down my fifth coffee of the morning...damn sleeping pills.

As it turned out, we needn't have been in such a hurry. The weather was beautiful across the country and the plane was sitting at the gate...cleaned, fueled, and ready to roll. Sometimes the travel gods are with you. We did the usual boarding kabuki dance...Melanie went in first, while I suffered jokes about dress codes and my "tasteful" plastic bag brief case. And that was from the cabin crew, lord only knows what my fellow passengers were thinking. Somehow I suspect the air marshal was moved to sit behind me, again.

Have I mentioned that flying with Melanie is a relatively dull affair? My wife suffers air, auto, and seasickness. As a result, she downs two motion sickness pills immediately before takeoff. Known to induce sleep in even the brawniest truck driver, these little white dots render Melanie comatose for approximately half of every flight. The remainder of her conscious time is spent watching whatever movie the airline offers. I suffer no such problem, and have little interest in most of the entertainment fair. I use flight time to read and do some writing. Makes for a quiet trip…normally. This was not the case today. As soon as she came out of the drug-induced trance, Melanie began fretting. "What if she doesn't like us?" "What if Alfred has told her something untoward?" "What if she thinks we are too snobby?" "What if…"

It does me no good to argue to the contrary during such events. Melanie likes to worry. In fact, I'm convinced she would find something to worry about even if the planets and stars were perfectly aligned in our favor. I've also learned to appreciate some of this behavior. Because she worries, Melanie is always prepared with directions, maps and reservations. She also handles the checkbook and deals with all legal issues. It's good to be me…except when the worrying involves the uncontrollable. Then I can simply offer reassurance and hope the motion sickness pills kick back in.

At least Melanie does not have to worry the arrival time. Blessed with a tailwind, we are slated to touchdown 30 minutes ahead of schedule. Whew. Barring unforeseen traffic woes…always a possibility in LA…or getting lost, we should be in Alfred's office 45 minutes ahead of the meeting. I should have left off getting lost. In LA Melanie does the driving, and she does not get lost. That feat is left for the male member of the family—me.

And so it is we find ourselves standing outside Alfred's office door at 0915. With no one in sight. Why we keep thinking Alfred is actually going to be on time—less early—for any meeting is beyond me. Alfred's version of 10 o'clock seems to take place approximately 30 minutes after that event has occurred on everyone else's schedule. We go for a walk. Better to burn off the nervous energy before the session. But now Melanie even has me worrying—what happens if the young lady is not impressed…how will we handle another disappointment? Maybe I should have listened to Melanie and worn socks with the loafers. Alas, too late now. At 10:25am Alfred walks us in for the first of several nerve-racking sessions.

Chapter X
Meeting the Birth-Mom to Be

Denial ain't just a river in Egypt.

—Mark Twain

My friends and acquaintances will tell you I am highly risk acceptant. On more than one occasion I have informed Melanie that my last words are likely to be "watch this." I would also be quick to note, however, that I am not a candidate for the Darwin Award—an annual compilation of male fatal acts of stupidity. I have no interest in fishing with dynamite, juggling engaged chainsaws, or arguing with the Secret Service. Instead, I enjoy determining and repeat testing a motorcycle's top speed, and have been known to shake and then open unmarked packages that appear on our doorstep. Furthermore, I am a self-confessed extrovert. Teaching before an auditorium with 500 students is not daunting; it's downright amusing. They haven't heard all my stories…Melanie has, and maintains little interest in reruns.

All that said, once we were seated in Alfred's dusty conference room—the aging law books had still not been moved—even I was beginning to suffer a nervous twitch. My attire wasn't the problem. In accordance with Melanie's very specific guidance I was dressed in a pair of pressed kakis and a starched, long-sleeved dress shirt. (Look Ma, no tattoos…or at least no immediately visible tattoos.) I had ditched the clogs for a pair of loafers and was even wearing a belt. This was no mean feat, as the change from urban shabby to LA chic had occurred in the front seat of the car as Melanie raced for Alfred's office. (I'm not bashful…you want to watch a grown man change clothes while you surf LA rush hour traffic, feel free…Melanie has been known to use the distracted drivers as a means of gaining lane advantage.)

Furthermore, it wasn't for want of something to say. Alfred had provided a few thoughts on appropriate topics and Melanie stepped me through a few other options. So I wasn't about to engage in a show-stopping verbal gaffe. No, I was nervous because we were about to come face-to-face with the young lady who would potentially bring our son or daughter into the world. That's right, I said son or daughter. At this point in the process we did not know the baby's sex. Mom, Alfred informed us, wasn't holding out; she simply had not received any prenatal care. So asking questions about the baby's gender was out. As were questions about the young lady's parents. Mom and Dad had tossed her out of the house.

Seems Tiffany, the prospective birth mother, had dealt with this pesky pregnancy problem by denying anything was wrong. Rather than seek the counsel of grown adults—what teenager would do that?—she opted not to tell anyone. She also took to dressing in floppy sweat suits as a means of disguising the obvious physical signs. This charade continued through the first six and a half months of the gestation period….and then the whole plan came asunder. Tiffany's mother, with three children of her own, knew a bit about how one appears when pregnant. She also developed a significant suspicion about her 16 year-old daughter's amazing appetite. Tiffany, like the young lady in Tucson, weighed about 100lbs and was best described as petite…even at this point in the game. So her sudden interest in candy bars and second helpings likely was viewed with more than casual interest. In today's America, no teenage girl actually wants to gain weight. Heroin addict thin remains the desired look…at least among 16 year-old females.

At any rate, Tiffany took to avoiding her mother by spending time with an aunt. The aunt, a legal secretary, had her own hands full with two young children and thus did not question the reason for her niece's dowdy appearance. In fact, Tiffany's sudden interest in hanging about with the aunt's rambunctious charges was a real god send...never look a gift horse in the mouth. The aunt did, however, also made note of her niece's appetite. And began making jokes about Tiffany's being pregnant. I suspect Tiffany found these jests terribly unfunny, but when one is hiding from reality—or a potentially outraged mother—even bad humor is better than facing the music.

So, Tiffany managed to make it for 26 weeks without spilling the beans or more appropriately, confessing to a bun in the oven. Finally, though, mom caught on. Less than a week before our meeting with Tiffany, the girl's mother dragged her to a doctor. I'm not a physician, but one look at the young woman and even I could diagnose the malady. "You, dear, are with child, pregnant, or...to use 16 year-old language...knocked up." Seems the doctor in Bakersfield came to a similar conclusion. Good to know one can at least count on the medical profession to assess and treat the obvious. Everything else requires four tests and at least three different medications.

To say that the news did not sit well with Tiffany's mother is an understatement; she flew off the hinges...which certainly helps explain why the young lady had opted for denial over confession. (Ainsley should beware; Melanie is not going to allow her teenager to suddenly take up baggy attire and a new diet without a lot of pointed questions. I never escape from these interrogations without divulging state secrets. Ainsley will be 'fessing up to everything a lot sooner than 6 months into the story.) Anyway, without any further discussion, Tiffany's mother marched the young lady straight to the nearest abortion clinic.

Eric C Anderson

I have a lot of respect for doctors who still practice abortion. They are providing a service that generates a very real risk to their own lives. Given humankind's tendency to engage in foolish behavior—and realize they are poorly suited to be parents—this service will be necessary into the foreseeable future. We as a society just need to come to this conclusion before the religious zealots drive women back into seeking dangerous alternatives. Ok, ok, I'll get off my soap box and back to the story.

Tiffany's mother walked her daughter up to the front desk of the clinic and insisted on seeing a doctor straight away. Eventually, the doctor meets them and examines Tiffany. Here's the good news...for us, not Tiffany. The doctor explained to Tiffany's mother that abortion simply was not an option in the sixth month of pregnancy; Tiffany needs an obstetrician, not an abortion provider. Tiffany's mother lost all semblance of rationality. After pleading for a second opinion...and being told no one was going to act on her demand for an abortion...she apparently commenced to screaming and then stomped out of the building.

The mother-to-be was driven home, told to pack, and was promptly delivered to the aunt we met a few short pages ago. This seemingly well-grounded woman with some experience in the legal profession knew there were options beyond abortion. Specifically, she knew about private adoptions and the financial assistance Tiffany might be offered by carrying the child to term for wanting parents. A few minutes on Google and Alfred's name and number were sitting on the screen. And so we arrived at the moment Melanie and I had been sweating...a sit down with a birth mother.

Enter Tiffany and her aunt from stage left. Tiffany turns out to be about 4 foot 10 inches, very petite, and very pregnant. Her aunt, a mid-30s blond, is clearly in charge of the young lady. She selected seats across the table from Melanie and me, scanned each of us carefully, and then offered introductions. So far so good. Tiffany came across as articulate and bright, but short on small talk.

In retrospect this makes good sense, how would you feel if parked in the middle of four adults all because of a few beers and bad judgment? My bet is that "chatty" is not the prevailing emotion.

Alfred, having been in this situation on multiple occasions, came to the rescue. According to California state law he had a number of questions that Tiffany needed to answer. The first requires no explanation—"you come here freely and aware of the consequences of your decision?" "Yes." Before Alfred can get to the next item the aunt chimed in. "We have talked about adoption at length and believe this is the best decision for Tiffany and the baby." Hmmmm, I hope this is not an indication the aunt is so overbearing that we will never hear from Tiffany—the person who really has to be comfortable with this momentous decision.

Next question: "How did you come to be in this situation?" Whoever put this item on the list must have really enjoyed watching young women squirm. Tiffany was clearly pained by the prospect of having to fill us in on the gory details. "I went to two parties, drank beer, had sex, and got pregnant." OK, so we're not going to get the Harlequin Romance version of the story. Fine with me. I don't need to hear more. Tiffany's predicament was readily apparent.

"Do you know who the father is?" Alfred was actually ticking off the questions on his checklist. "No."

Ok, allow me to sidetrack for a moment. In modern America, a father's rights when it comes to pregnancy and adoption are… well, a legal ballet dance. Before any adoption can go forward the parental rights of both the biological mother and father must be terminated. Easy enough with the pregnant woman who wants give up her child, but much more complicated when it comes to the biological father. While it used to be that unmarried biological fathers had few rights concerning their potential off-spring (and still don't in Utah), for the most part, modern law protects biological fathers in a manner similar to that of biological mothers. So when a biological father is out of the picture, or unknown, lawyers have to jump through hoops to make sure his rights are properly terminated and he can't come back later to claim the child.

The law presumes a married man is the biological father of a child born to his wife. Given the frequency with which unmarried partners now live together, there is also generally a presumption that a man who lives with a woman is the father of any child born to her while they live together. But when a child is conceived out of wedlock or when the mother is not living with a man with whom she has a sexual relationship…as in Tiffany's case—there is no presumption of paternity. Paternity is established only if a biological father signs a document declaring himself the child's father.

Where Dad can potentially be identified, generally he simply signs a document relinquishing his parental rights. If he can't be identified, a birth mother who seeks to place a child for adoption attests that she is unable to name the father. A court then terminates the unnamed father's paternal rights. In some states, however, the law requires that advertisements be placed in a local newspaper indicating that the birth mother is pregnant and requesting that any putative father come forward and identify himself. After a designated waiting period—30 days to 6 months—if no father comes forward, the court terminates the unidentified father's parental rights.

You can imagine how these ads read: "On 31 Nov 2008, a baby girl was born in LA to Tiffany X. The child is now up for adoption. If you believe you are the father and want to claim paternal rights, you must file paper work within the next 30 days." Or some such. Alfred assured us these ads can be run in local, minimal distribution, weeklies and that there is zero probability a potential father will come forward. Hell, if I was the typical 16 year-old male and thought I might be responsible for a pregnancy that would cost me a lot of time and money…you can damn well bet I would not be running into any courthouse. Presuming, of course, that I was even actually reading this kind of advertisement. Yup, I'm betting the odds were in our favor.

Melanie, however, was adamant we get this issue resolved. As someone familiar with the legal issues in adoption (she had written a law review article on the subject years earlier), she was painfully aware that some courts took this whole unidentified dads issue to absurd heights. As Melanie explained, there had been several well publicized cases in which courts had decided a father's rights to his biological child trumped a minor's right to remain in the care of stable, loving adoptive parents even years after the adoption had taken place. In an infamous Chicago, Illinois, case five-year old "Oscar" had been ripped from the parents who had adopted him at birth and returned to a biological father who had been unaware of the child's existence. Go figure. Melanie wasn't prepared to take any chances that anyone could ever take our adopted child away from us. And though such a possibility was remote at best, she was adamant that we take every possible legal precaution.

In the meantime, Tiffany's answer worked for Alfred and Melanie made a mental note to file all the appropriate paperwork as soon as possible. Me? Well, I thought the whole two party story was a crock of crap. Tiffany knew who dad was. She was either protecting the young man as a result of puppy love or, and more likely, she wasn't going to admit who it was because his racial or ethnic identity might not be acceptable to her mother. Nope, Tiffany wasn't saying a thing. And we were done asking.

Alfred continued on down his list. "Please tell us if you have any family history of mental health issues or if you have health issues that could affect the long-term well-being of the unborn child." Tiffany stated there were no health concerns she could think of and declared she had always been in good shape. (I buy the latter, but was a little worried about the former. Given her mother's behavior I suspect one could make the case for mental health issues…or at least a history of big anger management problems. I was wise enough to keep my mouth shut.)

Now we come to the tough one. "How do you intend to support yourself until the child is born?" Tiffany didn't get a chance to even inhale before her aunt rejoined the conversation. "We are hoping the adoptive parents will be able to provide the money necessary for medical care, assorted requirements, and room and board." I should have seen this one coming given the fact Tiffany's mother had tossed her out of the house. Melanie certainly had expected the request; she didn't even take a deep breath when the aunt finished making this pitch. We both agreed.

"That finishes the prelims." Alfred seemed satisfied with the interview. He now turned to Tiffany. "Any questions you want to ask?" The young lady assumed a pained expression that broadcast "NO" loud enough for the office staff to hear outside the closed doors. Her aunt, on the other hand, seemed eager to begin an inquisition of the would-be adoptees. "Why do you want to adopt?" Melanie and I had fielded this one before. It was the equivalent of opening with a slow, underhanded pitch right across home plate. Melanie, par usual, offered the by-now canned response. "We believe we have much to offer a child and would like to return some of the opportunities we were afforded growing up." So far so good. The aunt clearly liked this response.

"How would you raise the child?" Hmmmm…good question. But likely not the time to discuss discipline (my mother favored the wooden spoon) or religion (the aunt could be a fundamentalist Christian for all we knew). Nope, this was the time for an official vanilla answer. "With a lot of love, family, and close friends." That line should be on a greeting card. It insults no one and can be sent to even the sappiest relative. The aunt nodded her head, but was issuing body language that suggested she wanted more specifics. Melanie complied. "We are old enough to understand how important it is to take time for a child. We will be going to all school events and any other activities our child desires to participate in. Furthermore, my family lives within a two hour drive and will want to be part of the child's life." This seemed to scratch the aunt's itch.

"What about education?" Back to lofting softballs. Have I mentioned my doctorate in political science? I know I've mentioned Melanie's law degree. You might say we have a thing for education. Or at least the lucrative income one can achieve as a result of indulging in years of higher education. Melanie summed up those observations less sarcastically. "We believe a good education is critical to a child's development, expect to send a child to college and likely graduate school and will send our child to the best schools available." There goes my retirement Cadillac and thoughts of acquiring a second motorcycle in the foreseeable future. My dreams of a sailboat moored on the Potomac were also clearly just that—dreams. Tuition bills here we come.

My musings remained unspoken. Reasonably, the aunt appeared pleased with this response. Melanie was on a roll and we were coming up smelling of roses. This is why one hires an attorney to stand before a judge and jury. The lawyer knows how to phrase things in a manner that plays well with the audience at hand. I typically land up insulting someone. This why I open all my classes with a warning that my language is foul and that I am not politically correct—and have no desire to fix either issue.

Alfred stepped back in. "Any other questions for Eric and Melanie?" Tiffany looked at her aunt, her aunt looked at us. "No." Whew. I was worried for a moment that I would be asked to actually mutter a meaningful sentence. Seems Tiffany and I were off the hook. The conversation was being handled by the people who were actually paid to talk carefully for a living. "Alright." Alfred stood up. "Let's take a break for 15 minutes and let Tiffany do some thinking." Tiffany and her aunt exited the conference room with Alfred leading the charge. This left Melanie and I to stare and the books and wonder what would happen next.

Unwilling to sit in silence—another of my shortfalls—I tried small talk. "That seemed to go well." Melanie's response "I'm worried." As I well know, Melanie is always worried about one thing or another. I already knew where this particular worry was headed. "What if she doesn't like us?" See, I told you I knew where this conversation was headed. "She'll like us." "What makes you think that?" Melanie's retort would normally have caused me to search for words…I already had the answer in this case. "Because her aunt likes us. We didn't need to impress Tiffany; we needed to impress the aunt. You succeeded."

Melanie didn't seem to buy my theory, but for lack of evidence to the contrary chose to change the subject. "Where is Tiffany going to stay if she chooses us?" Uh, hadn't thought about that little wrinkle. Melanie, on the other hand, was already well down the path. "I suppose she could stay with us." At least I knew how to answer that idea. "Uh, no. We don't need a pregnant 16 year-old living with us. At this rate we could land up with two children—Tiffany and the baby." Melanie didn't seem convinced by my logic, but was not in the mood to argue. "Alfred likely has ideas." I nodded my head north and south in agreement, and began an aimless leafing through one of the dusty law books. My efforts at small talk were not generating progress and I have learned that Melanie prefers silence in high pressure situations.

As it turns out, we didn't have to wait long. About five minutes after departing to discuss our parenting potential, Tiffany, the aunt, and Alfred tromped back into the conference room. This time Tiffany began the conversation. "I would like you to be the mother and father of my child." Alright! We had crossed the Rubicon—a fancy way of saying the point of no return—and were destined to officially become mom and dad! The immediate feeling is like scratching the film off an instant lottery card and discovering

Adopting Ainsley

the state now owes you $10,000. It doesn't happen often, but when it does one is ready to dance a little jig around the shiny brass pole. Whoops, wrong metaphor in this situation, but you get the idea… we were quietly elated.

Hugs all around the room. Melanie got a little teary-eyed, and the four of us agree to head out for lunch. While we're out I am silently hoping Alfred is not thinking about a liquid diet before all the paperwork is signed. He is looking rough around the edges today and might feel better after a little hair of the dog. No such option in our world. One does not take a pregnant 16 year-old out for a celebratory drink at any time of the day. That said, a glass of white wine seemed appropriate…a thought I suspect Melanie shared but was not going to vocalize.

"Any recommendations for a lunch spot?" Melanie was already planning our escape. Alfred waved his hand in the direction of the movie studio across the street and suggested we try any one of the swank eateries about a block up from the law offices. Wonderful, an opportunity to dine al fresco with the true beautiful people of LA. Neither Tiffany nor her aunt expressed objections, so we headed for the door.

I may have failed to mention Alfred's office is in Culver City, a part of LA dedicated to Sony Studios. Unlike much of LA, Culver City is actually walkable and the local drivers do not appear intent on running down the first wayward pedestrian that crosses a road without looking. You think I'm kidding. LA actually hands out a large number of jaywalking tickets to prevent such accidents. The city is a Mecca for drivers…at least when traffic is moving…it has no such aspirations for people who think walking is a suitable form of transportation. "Get in your car and drive" should be LA's unofficial motto.

Nonetheless, we walked the three blocks to lunch. It just seemed like a good idea and a means of possibly generating a little chit-chat with Tiffany. No joy. But her aunt talked up a storm, largely about Tiffany's living arrangements in the coming months. As it turns out, Tiffany was free to return home once the baby was safely in our hands. Her mother simply did not want to deal with the embarrassment of a pregnant daughter—family pride or loss of face was at the root of the banishment—and so had requested the aunt seek living arrangements for the young lady. Furthermore, Tiffany was prohibited from contacting anyone at home until the baby was delivered…this silence was to be attributed to participation in a semester abroad program. (Uh, to where? Antarctica?)

Seems all of this had been shared with Alfred's staff the day before we arrived and they had come up with a solution. Tiffany would be staying with a relative of Alfred's receptionist. The relative was an older woman who lived in Las Vegas. She had taken on this role in the past and was already set to assume responsibility for Tiffany's care and feeding—for a monthly fee of $1,500. You already know who's paying that bill…yup, the adoptive parents. I was beginning to think a lunch of fast food and water or maybe a glass of cheap box wine was in order given the new fiscal austerity plan I was envisioning to offset all the adoption expenses.

We walked into a nice looking bistro where one seemed likely to bag a sighting of one Hollywood celebrity or another. I did a quick look around…no one famous I recognized. Not that I'm a good gauge for such issues. Meryl Streep could be sitting next to me on a trans Atlantic flight and I probably wouldn't be able to identify her. We noshed on the salads while basking in the early fall sun. The aunt shared tales of child rearing and working for an attorney who had died at the office.

Searching for more interesting topics, I tried again to lure Tiffany into talking. "What are you going to do about school for the next couple of months?" She stared at her salad and apparently attempted to divine what might be the appropriate answer. "Oh, I'll sign up for a correspondence program." The silent child speaks! "What are you going to study?" If she had answered biology I would have gagged on my wilted-leaf arugula salad. (True foofoo LA food...what's the matter with burgers? Specifically, good old-fashioned beef burgers, spare me the soybean silliness. That stuff is cat food for humans.) Tiffany saved me. "History, English, and maybe geometry."

Typical stuff for a 16 year-old. Or so I thought. I hadn't been 16 for more than 30 years, so what did I know about the subject? "What else are you going to do to pass time?" "Watch TV." Well, Tiffany was clearly an American child. I suppose she could have said play video games, but that seems an occupation monopolized by boys. Girls appear content to sit back without trying to shoot or kill something every 30 seconds.

Lunch ended without any major *faux pas* on my part. We made our way back to Alfred's office for a final round of paper signing and establishment of an account to take care of Tiffany's needs for the coming 10 weeks. Good old Alfred. He could not be relied upon to respond to emails or phone calls, but when it came to money, he was all over the situation. By the time we returned from lunch his staff had assembled—in triplicate—a full billing statement and printed out forms where we guaranteed a steady flow of cash sufficient to raise a family of four.

He also had devised a means of covering Tiffany's medical bills and birth-related expenses. Using his connections in Las Vegas, Alfred was already drafting the documents necessary to make Tiffany a ward of the state. By declaring her jobless and homeless, Alfred was able to qualify Tiffany for medical treatment via Temporary Aid to Needy Families. (This is the program we used to call Aid to Families with Dependent Children.) While this may seem sneaky or illegal, I am informed that is not the case. Tiffany's parents had no health insurance, and as she was not related to us she did not fall under our coverage. In fact, Tiffany's situation revealed many of the problems in our health care system. She didn't qualify for prenatal care, but an emergency room would be unable to turn her away when she gave birth or if she developed any serious problems—problems that regular medical care might have prevented in the first place. In any event, under Nevada law, Tiffany could eventually fall back on taxpayer subsidized health providers. We approved Alfred's plan, given the rest of our expenses I envisioned a diet of bologna sandwiches for the foreseeable future.

What was the final plan? In short, it worked like this. We were paying for Tiffany and her aunt's plane tickets to Las Vegas. We then were to pay Tiffany's room and board, provide a monthly allowance, and cover phone bills for the young lady. Finally, we were to ante up for a one-time set of expenses—linens, towels, toiletries, etc—and put $500 aside for maternity outfits. Damn, this pregnant teen thing was a lucrative business. Melanie wrote Alfred a check for $5,000.

We dropped Tiffany and her aunt off at the airport. Tiffany remained verbally incommunicado, but I did notice she was busily texting someone through the entire duration of our drive. Figuring she was not speaking with her mother or any school mates—remember, Tiffany was officially out of the country—the analyst in me leapt to a single conclusion. The wayward boyfriend—aka the biological father. I later pointed this out to Melanie…who seemed a little surprised, but not terribly concerned. "The father's rights have been legally addressed." That was the sum total of her observation.

I don't remember where we stayed that night. I know it was cheap because a blinking neon light served to illuminate the room for most of the night. That was but one indication. A very lumpy bed, a carpet that required one wear shoes when heading for the bathroom, and a décor screaming 1972 were other signs this was not the Ritz Carlton. Ok, so the Ritz was out. But look at the bright side. In 10 short weeks we would be parents—free to change diapers and begin the process of molding a new human in our very own image. I fell asleep wondering when I should introduce Melanie to the idea of a tattoo for our future munchkin.

Chapter XI
Travels to Las Vegas

In Nevada, for a time, the lawyer, the editor, the banker, the chief desperado, the chief gambler, and the saloon-keeper, occupied the same level in society, and it was the highest. The cheapest and easiest way to become an influential man and be looked up to by the community at large, was to stand behind a bar, wear a cluster-diamond pin, and sell whisky. I am not sure but that the saloon-keeper held a shade higher rank than any other member of society.

—Mark Twain

October was turning into a busy month. With Tiffany safely ensconced in Las Vegas, Melanie began to worry about the young lady's happiness. Despite her tough-as-nails reputation, Melanie has a soft side. I occasionally catch her getting teary-eyed in movies...and woe unto the being she catches mistreating a puppy. So I should not have been surprised to discover she was already contemplating when it would be appropriate to spend some time with Tiffany. Melanie figured this would help reassure Tiffany and alleviate the loneliness associated with her banishment from Bakersfield. I figured just escaping Bakersfield would be sufficient to meet the agenda—by god, Tiffany was in Las Vegas...what else could a salient being possibly desire?

Melanie assured me that this enthusiasm for all things Las Vegas was likely not shared by a pregnant 16 year-old who had limited access to spending money. The casinos were out—as were the associated free drinks. Tiffany had expressed no interest in the high desert. And given her condition, sitting by the pool in a skimpy bathing suit was ill-advised. Young men were likely to flee in fear of impending responsibility and pregnancy was not going to do much to flatter her figure. Confronted with that argument, I had to surrender to the logic of Melanie's position. Tiffany likely wanted company…and probably wanted to learn more about us.

The astute reader has probably already surmised Melanie and I have different perspectives when it comes to Las Vegas. Melanie is convinced that Las Vegas is best viewed from a plane passing over Nevada at 35,000 feet. She is not a fan of crowds, smoke-filled rooms, and tacky-hotels bedecked with themes like pirates and circuses. She will admit that Las Vegas is host to a number of fine restaurants, but would then hasten to contend similar fare can be had much closer to home without suffering any of the indignities listed above.

I, on the other hand, think Las Vegas is a wonderful escape from reality. While gambling has never done much for my soul—why throw money in slot machines when owning a sailboat will accomplish the same feat? At least with the sailboat one has an inkling of where the cash is being wasted…the same cannot be said of the one-armed bandits. I do, however, enjoy the people watching (visit a casino at 3 am…you'll never believe what goes wandering through the maze of machinery and card tables), find the free drinks delightful (but very watered down), and like running the bike on open highways where law enforcement can typically be spotted beyond the range of any existing speed detection devices.

How much do I like Vegas? Well, I lived there in the mid-90s. Over the course of a couple of years I discovered the joys of snow skiing in the morning and then being dragged behind a boat in the afternoon. Yup. One can drive up Mount Charleston and put in a few hours on the slopes before heading to Lake Meade for a cold beer and swimsuit. The hiking is simply outstanding—so long as rattle snakes and 110 degrees don't seem an imposition. And, best of all, there are several local bars that firmly believe one should only be allowed in the parking lot atop a Harley Davidson. Automobiles and Japanese crotch rockets are out. Yeah, I

Adopting Ainsley

like Vegas...and have infrequently reminded Melanie that I would be happy to move back in the not so distant future. My wife claims she will visit, but suggests I would be more likely to remain in good stead by planting my feet firmly east of the Potomac. The things we men will suffer in order to maintain happiness at home.

Knowing this to be the case, you can bet I was impressed with Melanie's willingness to survive another long plane flight and then wrestle with the unwieldy traffic jam Las Vegas has become. She clearly wanted to ensure Tiffany was comfortable and adjusting to her present predicament. Furthermore, Melanie was talking about making two or three trips to Las Vegas over the coming months... all before the baby was even slated for delivery.

Thinking of the baby, two days after Tiffany arrived in Las Vegas we learned the sex of our child to-be. Dutifully following up on everyone's recommendation, Tiffany had her first prenatal examination. After determining she was indeed pregnant—see, I told you we should retain faith in the American medical system—the doctor set about the standard set of evaluations, including an ultrasound. Amazing thing those ultrasound examinations. Despite a layer of skin, internal organs, and amniotic fluid, the medical gurus can discern the presence or absence of some very crucial bits of anatomy. A fancy way of saying, they can tell you if that bulge is a boy or a girl—or even twins. We were going to have a daughter! Melanie and I sighed in relief and went out to dinner.

This bit of celebration, I should note, came with its own unique burden. While we had long desired to have a girl, neither Melanie nor I had done serious thinking about an appropriate moniker, call sign...uh, name, for the child. You would think we would have accomplished this bit of crucial homework prior to our Tucson adventure. You would be wrong. Unwilling to rush to conclusions before we knew the sex of our child in-waiting, the two of us had engaged in that all-American sport of procrastination. We figured we would likely have months to come up with a name.

Needless to say, this tactic drew some pressure on the home front. The grandparents wanted to know what the new member of the family would be called…and preferred to have an answer sooner rather than later. This was particularly true of my parents, who have confronted an interesting cultural gap on this particular issue. As I have previously mentioned, my brother's wife is from India. In her culture it is not unusual to hold off on naming a child for up to 12 months after delivery. The cause for this delay is not irrational. In a country where death was historically common in children younger than 1, parents avoided even greater grief by not declaring a name before the infant was nearly a toddler. This may make sense in India, not so much with my mother, who resides just north of Seattle. She named my brother's first son Bubba long before a quarter of the designated period had elapsed.

My mother, like Melanie, is not shy about expressing her opinions. And so one can accurately conclude I was under considerable pressure to conform with Western conventions. (I suspect this pressure was further increased by the fact it took my brother and his wife approximately 14 months to announce a name for their second off-spring…you would think they would have learned after the first experience.) To ward off the questions, we periodically tossed out ideas.

Melanie's first suggestion, Summer Sloan, drew the following response from my side of the table. "Great name for a stripper, not sure we want to suggest such career options early in any child's upbringing." I thought it was a great retort. Melanie was not amused. She likes summer—the season and the name—and was willing to push back a little. "It would at least be uncommon." OK, Melanie had me on this one, how were we to know if we were about to condemn the poor girl to being Summer 1, Summer 2, or Summer 3 during the first day of school. Lord knows my parents didn't worry about this…you have no idea how many people named Eric are in my age group—including Melanie's ex husband.

Adopting Ainsley

As it turns out, the Social Security Administration actually maintains a web site that lists the most popular names for any given year between 1879 and the present. All you have to do is go on line and begin surfing. It is, by the way, a great place to come up with options when you are sick of suggestions from friends and relatives. You think I'm kidding? Watch this.

The 10 most popular names for boys and girls in 1879:

1	John	Mary
2	William	Anna
3	James	Emma
4	Charles	Elizabeth
5	George	Minnie
6	Frank	Margaret
7	Joseph	Ida
8	Thomas	Alice
9	Henry	Bertha
10	Robert	Sarah

Neat trick...but a little disappointing. It would appear parents in 1879 were no more imaginative than parents in 1929:

Eric C Anderson

1	Robert	Mary
2	James	Betty
3	John	Dorothy
4	William	Helen
5	Charles	Margaret
6	Richard	Doris
7	Donald	Barbara
8	George	Ruth
9	Joseph	Shirley
10	Edward	Patricia

Or in 2009:

1	Jacob	Isabella
2	Ethan	Emma
3	Michael	Olivia
4	Alexander	Sophia
5	William	Ava
6	Joshua	Emily
7	Daniel	Madison
8	Jayden	Abigail
9	Noah	Chloe

Time to break with the paradigm. Our daughter was not going to join a sea of Jennifers or a gaggle of Marys. Nope. We wanted something unique. A name that would stand out in a crowd and yet not be culturally or ethnically defining. (Melanie and I were well aware of the fact employers screen resumes looking for particular kinds of names. If your parents chose Latifa the folks

Adopting Ainsley

in HR are already betting you are African American. If you come up as Jose—well, the bad jokes about all things Latin and South American have already begun.)

So here's where my eclectic interest in economics comes to play. I have always been a fan of Brooksley Born. I frequently contend Brooksley Born should be a household name in today's America. A graduate of Stanford Law School, Ms Born served as the chairwoman of the Commodities Futures Trading Commission (CFTC) from 26 August 1996 to 1 June 1999. For those of you who don't think the *Wall Street Journal* is required reading—aka, a normal American citizen—CFTC is the federal agency tasked with overseeing the futures and commodity options markets. Yawn, boring stuff...with one minor exception. The CFTC could have saved us from the 2008-2009 recession had Congress and Bill Clinton been willing to listen to Brooksley Born.

You see, Brooksley—I'll be bold and pretend we are on a first-name basis—recognized the risk inherent in the growing market for financial derivatives, and called for regulation of this little-understood corner of our economy. Her bid to reel in the greed-mongers of Wall Street ran head long into Alan Greenspan, Robert Rubins, Lawrence Summers and Bill Clinton. This good-old-boys club figured they knew better than the little lady from Stanford...and dismissed her concerns as unnecessary oversight cost that would create needless turmoil in the marketplace. Well, we now know who was right...and it sure wasn't Greenspan, Rubins, Summers or Clinton. They should have been listening to Brooksley. The American economy would be significantly better off today had they not been so damn Adam Smith sure of themselves.

Enough of the history lesson. Back to the name game. In addition my fascination with Brooksley Born's foresight, I liked the alliteration that came with her name. It just rolls off one's tongue, and sticks in the mind. I'm betting no one had to ask Brooksley to repeat her name more than twice, after that it was captured and filed. Exactly what a parent desires for a child in whom they harbor high ambitions—or at least great earning potential. Come on, there are no famous Eric Andersons. Even adding the middle initial to my signature block does little to help audience recall. We were not going to make that mistake with our daughter.

This seemed like a water-tight argument from my side of the bed. Melanie was still not convinced. "How about Summer Anderson?" See, I told you summer was stuck in her mind. "No, sounds like the off-spring of two hippies." I may have poor taste in airline attire and furniture, but I will not be confused for an aging hippy. I do not place daises in the barrel of a gun or wear tie-dye t-shirts. Leave that tree-hugging stuff to the hybrid driving crowd. I prefer steak with my potatoes, not tofu and watercress. Melanie ignored my tirade about 1960s relics and suggested we go back to considering the options.

I have to admit this was becoming a frustrating consumption of my feeble brain power. I lost track of the number of options that were rejected because dad, me, would have to bring a piece of paper to school with his daughter's name so as to ensure I spelled same correctly. (Spell check has saved me from complete literary obscurity. Without this automatic option my emails and letters would be a source of amusement and confusion.) I can't spell and didn't want to spend the rest of my life having to check on the proper letter ordering for Samantha or Rebbecca…or is that Rebecca?

Fortuitously, Melanie saved us from a life of indecision. We have a habit of visiting bookstores while waiting for movie theaters to open. Full disclosure is in order here. When it comes to bookstores I am stuck in a bit of a rut. Melanie will peruse all the tables and consider the latest new titles. She wanders through different sections and is apt to make serendipitous discoveries. I am less open-minded. Upon entering any establishment engaged in the peddling of published materials I immediately aim for the East

Adopting Ainsley

Asia section. Phooey on that literature stuff, I'm looking to see if there is anything new to read on China.

Over the years Melanie has become accustomed to this narrow-minded behavior and often will randomly pick something to pursue until I reemerge from the inevitably dust-ridden section of my choosing. On this particular day, she had found a text that provided 10,000 options for naming one's child. I don't know how many pages she had already consumed…or upon what letter of the alphabet she started the search…but when I found her sitting on the floor next to the shelves of child-rearing advice, she had come up with a suggestion. Ainsley.

Ainsley…hmmm. According to the text, Ainsley, a derivative of a Scottish surname—means a hermitage in or at the clearing in the woods. Yeah, yeah. I really wonder who spends time looking up the meaning of their name—probably the same people who wear tie-dye t-shirts, plant daisies, and drive old VW vans. I was more curious about the popularity of this particular moniker. As it turns out, Ainsley is relatively obscure. Even though it is considered suitable for a boy or girl, Ainsley rarely breaks through 800 on the list of 1,000 most popular names. Melanie liked that exclusivity… but I was sold on the pairing…Ainsley Anderson…damn, that was almost as good as Brooksley Born. I was hooked.

Now a few of you are going to start wondering about my sexist attitude. Why Anderson? Why not Sloan? Good question. Melanie started life as a Togman. As in Melanie Togman. A fine name, but she wasn't partial to the guttural g—and always having to spell it out for everyone. Melanie was looking for something that was a bit smoother. I'm sure that's not the whole reason she married Eric Sloan, but when they parted company she kept the name. Melanie's ex now has three children—though his second wife didn't take the name—and she felt there were enough Sloans in that brood—so why not go with Anderson? I argued there is no shortage of Andersons, but she was insistent. So Ainsley Anderson it was.

Yes, yes. I see there are still skeptics in the audience. In the back of your mind the thought lingers…that knuckle-dragger just kept nagging until he won the decision. So here's my further defense on the issue of names. When Melanie and I discussed marriage, we both considered the option of changing last names to come up with a common pairing. The hyphenated silliness was out…Anderson-Sloan or Sloan-Anderson will not fit in the space offered for job applications or on a military uniform. Melanie was adamant she was keeping her name for business purposes and I had this whole publishing peskiness to deal with. Nonetheless, I offered to become Eric C. Sloan. Melanie nixed the suggestion. She had already been married to one Eric Sloan, there was no need to go for a second. So we each kept our last names and proceeded like any modern couple.

Ainsley's middle name offered one more opportunity. Another issue upon which I think much too much time is expended. One is either mortified by their middle name or simply comes to believe it is nothing more than an initial. I know mine is Curt—for my grandfather—but it has been nothing more than "C" for as long as I can remember. Of course, if a child hates her first name, there is always the chance she can tolerate the middle one and can then easily switch to that. So I asked Melanie what we should choose to fill this seemingly mandatory position. Summer was in after all.

Resolving the great name game took us until Columbus Day weekend. This three-day holiday has traditionally served to mark my last great motorcycle trip of the season. Grab an extra pair of jeans, two changes of underwear, a credit card and head for the highway. Not this year. My father had just undergone the first of two knee replacements—they fixed the other one a year later—and my mother was looking for company and someone to help with completing a number of chores prior to winter. I volunteered, and thus was headed for Port Townsend, Washington. Melanie, on the other hand, was about to make her first trip to Las Vegas.

Adopting Ainsley

Melanie had been working hard to develop a rapport with Tiffany. The two of them spoke on the phone three or four times a week and Melanie had made clear Tiffany was free to call at any hour of the day or night. My exposure to this dialogue was limited to small talk at dinner and a once-a-week conversation with Tiffany. I simply could not break the code on getting the young lady to speak...and found our conversations were largely a one-sided dialogue, with yours truly providing most of the volume.

Sensing that Tiffany was more than a little frightened and lonely, Melanie had offered to head to Las Vegas to spend a few days with the birth-mom to be. Ever the careful planer, Melanie had made dinner reservations and studied guidebooks for attractions appropriate for a teen-age girl—few and far between in Sin City. I thoughtfully recommended she also consider attending one of Tiffany's favored new films, but given the young lady's penchant for horror flicks Melanie opted to pass on that suggestion.

Melanie has no stomach for scary or violent movie scripts. She will actually sit on the couch and cover her face with a pillow when such material appears on TV. When some of our friends invited us to see *No Country for Old Men,* Melanie hid under her coat for nearly the entire film. I was well aware of her aversion to slasher flicks...but, hey, was just trying to help with the bonding process.

In addition to planning ahead, Melanie had recruited her sister, Kimberly, to join her on the trip. As someone who specializes in working HR issues and has been a career coach (though Melanie remains convinced her true calling would have been writing sentimental greeting cards for Hallmark), Kimberly has the ability to open and maintain a conversation with almost anyone. As best I could tell this skill was going to be essential in dealing with Tiffany. Between Melanie and Kimberly, I thought surely they would be able to tear the young lady away from her cell phone and get her to participate in something close to a conversation. I just worried the two of them might get on each other's nerves over the course of this long weekend. Like siblings across the planet, Melanie and her sister have a rotating love-hate relationship. Some days are up and others are not. Same could be said of the connection between me and my brother. Growing older diminishes the fires, but it sure doesn't extinguish all the flames.

With all that in mind, I headed for Dulles and Melanie drove up to Baltimore to catch our respective flights. I arrived in Seattle none the worse for wear and Melanie made it to Las Vegas. Melanie rented a mid-size sedan, I went in search of a toy. Years of experience have taught me that car rental firms typically have a hard time getting rid of their most expensive toys. Frugal travelers snatch up all the logical vehicles and leave the gas guzzlers and sports cars sitting on the lot…burning a hole in company balance sheets. Remember this the next time you go to rent a car at midnight on a Friday before a three-day weekend.

I drove out of the Seattle airport in an Audi A-8. The cheap version of this car goes for $75,000. The cheap version. Lord only knows what the fully loaded variant takes from one's checkbook. Powered by a 4.2 liter V-8, the Audi A-8 does 0-60 faster than my motorcycle. And the top end, well…even I couldn't find the top end. Not for want of trying or a lack of courage, but on the roads I was covering, there was simply no stretch empty or long enough for the Audi to wind out the speedometer. Instead I spent my time blasting out of intersections and passing in very small spaces. Cheap thrills, but at least they were thrills. I passed the weekend, helping my father navigate the stairs, and winterizing their house before they departed for their annual retreat to warmer climes.

Melanie found her weekend a little more difficult. She and Kimberly took Tiffany to see the Hoover Dam and the three of them ate out and got manicures and pedicures. But the conversation remained essentially nonexistent and even Kimberly was unable to break through Tiffany's rectitude. Melanie did note that Tiffany seemed to be well cared for and getting bigger. She also noticed the teen remained addicted to texting, strange since she had told us her mother had barred her from communicating with any friends back home. I remained suspicious this was the wayward father, but Tiffany did not give anything away. In fact, she really hadn't said much of anything.

Melanie, who is a fairly direct sort, found Tiffany's silence unnerving. She figured the girl had to be going through a rough time, having been banished to a Las Vegas suburb with no friends or family, or even school for companionship. She didn't want Tiffany to be miserable and she wanted to hear the young lady was still keen on giving the baby to us—that she wasn't having second thoughts about keeping the child. As unlikely as that prospect appeared given Tiffany's mother's strong views on the subject, after our experience in Tucson Melanie remained apprehensive.

Tiffany did, however, appear to appreciate the company Melanie and Kimberly offered and thanked them for coming out. She wanted to know if Melanie would return to join her for childbirth class. Glad no one was looking for my participation there. In other words, all seemed to be going well with our birth mother. At this rate we would be parents somewhere in the vicinity of Thanksgiving…a prospect that made all of the travel worth every minute of our time.

Chapter XII
A Little Rain Must Fall

...drag your thoughts away from your troubles—by the ears, by the heels, or any other way, so you can manage it; it's the healthiest thing a body can do.

—Mark Twain

Needless to say, the remainder of October vanished in a haze of falling leaves and last minute yard work. I set about the task of pulling out the annuals and planting a smattering of pansies. Hey, anyone can pull off the macho routine, it takes a real man to admit he likes a bit of color in front of the house throughout the seasons. To that end, in addition to serving as the household's chief bottle washer, I am the domicile's botanist. This is not a claim to bragging rights. On more than one occasion a neighbor has questioned whether the current collection of plants in the front yard was planned or came about by happenstance. Seems everyone's a critic...makes a guy all sensitive.

Issues with my fragile male ego aside, the end of October also brings about Melanie's least favorite holiday on Capitol Hill—Halloween. You remember Halloween. The holiday invented by candymakers and dentists. A holiday only a child or drunk college students can love. Or so I thought until moving onto Capitol Hill. Seems Halloween on Capitol Hill is a major event with a crowd fitting the moment. A more appropriate observation would be as follows. Capitol Hill sits across the river from Anacostia, one of Washington DC's poorest neighborhoods. Once a year the Anacostia residents get a chance to benefit from the largess only to be found in a neighborhood where most people don't have children, but do have high-paying jobs and understand the benefit of keeping the potential "tricksters" at bay through bribery.

Melanie had warned me about Halloween on Capitol Hill months ahead of my first experience with this event. She had warned me it was best to be out of town or at a long movie come the evening of 31 October. I registered this cautionary advice, but didn't really process the information. Knowing Melanie is no fan of crowds—regardless of size—I just figured she was exaggerating the "threat" and went back to contemplating my navel...still an "inny." I should have listened.

True to her word, as my first experience with Halloween on Capitol Hill began to pull into sight Melanie announced she was going to be at an out of town conference for the day prior and following the 31st. How convenient. This left me to do a modicum of planning—more specifically, to purchase a few bags of candy and a six-pack. When I showed Melanie my purchases she just laughed. "That's all you bought?" Hmmm. The three bags claimed to hold about 200 items, how many kids were going to descend on our house? As for the six-pack, go buy your own.

I went back to the store and came home with three more bags. Certainly that should meet demand. We're talking about Halloween...little children, not the plague of locusts. Turns out the latter is a better metaphor than the former. Oh, I was visited by little children accompanied by their mothers between 6 and 7pm. Then the real crowd rolled in. I've been alive a long time and seen a lot of strange things. But until that day I had never been accosted by high school students and adults engaged in trick-or-treating with backpacks to hold the loot. Trust me, when you open the door to find a crowd where the shortest participant is 6 feet tall generosity suddenly seems like a good idea. Why offer one piece of candy when 5 will do? I ran out of processed sugar products by 8.

Not wanting to appear a defenseless target for the tricksters, I grabbed a beer, lit a cigar, put the dog on a chain, and went out to sit on the door stoop. Even after informing the passing crowd that an even bigger hound was behind the closed drawbridge, I

Adopting Ainsley

was still asked for candy…or, even better yet, a spare beer. Damn, Halloween was never like this in central Wisconsin or even Hawaii. By 10pm I had run out of beer and cigars. The crowds were beginning to thin, so I headed upstairs for a few hours of nap time. No such luck. The door knockers continued until well after 11, and the truly diehard did not quit until well after midnight. Lesson learned, the next time Halloween rolled around I was also going to be at a conference or a very, very long movie.

As Halloween approached this year, we opted for the coward's route out. Rather than suffer the crowds and intimidation, Melanie suggested we head for Delaware to spend a night with her parents. Given the nature of their neighborhood—well groomed lawns with long driveways—it seemed almost certain we would not be witness to the mayhem that overwhelmed Capitol Hill. Think of it this way, Melanie's parents get to enjoy our company, the dog is spared howling all night long, and I save about 50 bucks that otherwise would have enriched Hershey's or some other industrial confectioner.

All of this is a long way of saying we made it to November relatively unscathed. Melanie continued to remain in near-daily communication with Tiffany, and I went about preparing my mind for the coming arrival of our very own small person. (To be more honest, I simply continued with my standard routine: gym, work, woodshop, dinner, TV, bed. Am I the average American, or am I the average American?) Meanwhile, Melanie was planning her next trip to Vegas and spent every spare moment looking at parenting books. Yet another phenomenon associated with having children later in life. Rather than learning child rearing skills by trial and error—just like good old Mom and Dad—we actually figured one could acquire knowledge through reading. Yeah, right. I was sticking to trial and error…Melanie could claim all the credit for book learning.

Eric C Anderson

Thinking of book learning and child-rearing, I almost forgot to mention the other activity that consumed several of our weekends…hiring a nanny. As almost everyone knows, the day of stay-at-home moms is long over. And I was not about to become a stay-at-home dad. Like Melanie, I enjoy the mental stimulus offered by dealing with adults; the prospect of 8 lonely hours locked up with a drooling infant did nothing for me. Interestingly, this put me 180 degrees out from my brother. Having made his fortune as an early Microsoft employee, my brother chose to stay home and raise his two sons. He claims the experience has been nothing but rewarding. As best I can tell, it cost him somewhere in the vicinity of 50 IQ points. The man who once spoke fluent computer geek now does little more than babble on about child safety concerns and the dangers of my secondhand cigar smoke. Nope, I had no plans to stay home with a newborn.

Not being made of money, we immediately considered daycare centers. Melanie looked up all the possible daycare options on Capitol Hill and in downtown Washington only to discover there were no daycare options. Don't get me wrong…there are children on Capitol Hill and there are daycare centers in Washington DC… but actually being able to use one of those facilities requires planning, a lot of planning.

It turns out the waiting lists for infant daycare in the District of Columbia stretch out 18 months or more. A couple should be thinking about daycare about the time of their first date. If you wait until sex rolls into the equation it's already too late. While as a nation we encourage mothers, particularly poor ones, to return to work, the reality is that daycare is not only unaffordable for many, it frequently is downright unavailable. Certainly, for anyone adopting an infant—who rarely know more than a few months ahead of time when the child will arrive—daycare is a non-starter.

So that put us in the market for a nanny. More specifically, that put us in the market for a nanny-share arrangement. A nanny-

Adopting Ainsley

share is the option one pursues when the cost of hiring one's own nanny would bankrupt the family. Not wanting to be financially bereft before the child reached college—we figured 4 years of university would offer plenty of opportunity lessons in scrimping and saving—Melanie went on-line to investigate nanny-share possibilities. Have I mentioned Melanie joined an internet group called "Mothers on the Hill" aka MOTH? Apparently she had been informed this semi-secretive organization (there is no Dads on the Hill) was a great source of useful data and mothering locker room stories. It is also the perfect place to search for parents equally concerned about how to afford junior's care once both parents return to the office.

After a few weeks of searching, Melanie came home and announced we were about to go meet our future nanny-share partners—Tom and Amber. Logistically, the pairing could not have been better. Tom and Amber live four blocks from our house, and Amber had recently given birth to tiny Riley. (Yes, yes, all children are tiny when they first appear…a fact I simply can't seem to fathom…I can, however, attest to the amount of racket one of those small packages can make with very little effort.) To our way of thinking this was perfect. Ainsley would have a sister and the four of us could get back to adult activities comfortable that our progeny were well cared for. Nice.

There was only one small problem. We had to hire a nanny. This is no light matter—as my significant other reminded me on multiple occasions. After all, the nanny was going to spend more waking hours with our daughters than any other person alive…including us. My personal thought was "whew," but managed to keep that sentiment confined to the inner voice. Fortunately, Melanie and Amber were all over this. In less than a week they managed to round up three qualified candidates and schedule a sequence of interviews.

Eric C Anderson

All I can say is that it's a good thing Tom and Amber are fluent Spanish speakers. With very few exceptions, all nannies now appear to come from Latin America. We had all agreed our daughters should grow up speaking a second language…it never dawned on me that I would have to do the same thing…or endlessly communicate in broken English. In turn, each of the nannies made their case and then we filled in the gaps with sparing questions. No shortage of qualifications, that was for sure. One would-be nanny had been a nurse, a second had raised four children of her own, and the third had been a nanny for over 20 years.

How do you sort the lot? Ask about discipline. One nanny suggested children needed a strong sense of right and wrong—to be instilled though lots of time out and lectures. (Ugh, reminded me of elementary school in the late 1960s…I spent a lot of time in very lonely places contemplating my latest misadventure.) The second nanny indicated discipline was instilled through hugs and endless attention. Right. That will work. Somehow handing a wayward child chocolate treats to induce proper behavior seemed more like training a dog than teaching the future leaders of America. It was the third nanny who came up with the right answer.

Children, she informed us, are best taught discipline though a combination of love, scolding, and short timeouts. Dr Benjamin Spock would be proud; his lessons continue to find practitioners more than 60 years after he first published *Baby and Child Care*. This nanny also expressed little concern about chasing two little girls and spoke of her last employers' children as though they were her very own. As best Tom and I could tell, she was perfect. Melanie and Amber were not so readily convinced. They insisted we go through yet another round of interviews just in case an even more perfect person was out there. Sigh. Not my idea of fun, but I was in no position to argue. Melanie had me on that whole "this person spends more waking hours with your daughter than anyone alive."

Adopting Ainsley

I will note, we did hire the third nanny, my instincts are still intact…but only after interviewing three more candidates. The second group was much less promising and consumed fewer hours of my diminishing free time, but it still made me feel like a second grader forced to sit through an opera. "Will this ever end? Will anyone notice if I sneak off to the bathroom and never return?"

Back to our story. By the time we finished dodging the Halloween madness and hiring a nanny Melanie was on the calendar for another trip to Las Vegas. In addition to the morale-building nature of this second trip, Melanie was heading for Sin City to attend a child-birthing class with Tiffany. I offered to spare her this whole ordeal by filling in, but was politely turned down at home and by the birth-mother to be. In retrospect this was a good thing. I mean, think about it. I was going to walk into a birthing class with someone who clearly looked young enough to be my daughter. All the soon-to-be dads would likely be wondering about how I was so fortunate, while all the soon-to-be moms would likely be silently condemning the old letch. Yeah, not my wisest offer. But one I felt compelled to make.

I have to admit my willingness to jump on a plane for 10 hours of flying and less than 36 hours of on-site time was not terribly high. Melanie's joy at taking on this mission was likely little better, but off she went with plans to attend a Cirque du Soleil performance and avoid horror films. (Cirque du Soleil, for the uninitiated, is a bit of performance art that combines dance, circus acts, and bizarre stage settings. I find the shows quite amusing, but I'm not sure Melanie is equally delighted. That said, the show had won Tiffany's approval, so to the Cirque they both would go.)

I never did get much in the way of a back brief concerning the child birth class. My guess, having seen movies depicting the travails of same, lots of lessons on breathing and a few scary films about the wonders to be found in a delivery room. I can also guess that Melanie urged Tiffany to consider painkillers and any other form of relief. Given Tiffany's petite size, a natural child birth was going to be hard…and she had already firmly ruled out a cesarean. I don't think the scar was Tiffany's fear. I suspect the cesarean got a thumbs down due to associated healing time. More than one woman has informed me a cesarean is no minor surgery and full recovery takes almost six weeks. Tiffany was making the right decision.

This gets us to middle of November. Only 2-3 more weeks before we would have our very own daughter! In a bid to share good news with friends and family, we invited Melanie's parents and her sister to Thanksgiving at our place. Normally, Melanie's parents host T-day…it's a Togman tradition. But this year Melanie's mom was suffering a nagging shoulder problem and was not up to the efforts required to feed a small army. We, on the other hand, were happy to do the cooking and show off the now well-stocked nursery. It was time to do a little bragging about all the preparations and enjoy a holiday before the sleepless nightmare began.

As much as we were willing to host Thanksgiving, all the guests were properly warned that a panic phone call from Las Vegas could bring all the festivities to a screeching halt. All heads nodded north to south in acknowledging this potential contingency and so we proceeded with the planning…and reviewing emails from Alfred's office concerning bills and their management of Tiffany's expense account. Nothing shocking on that front. Phone expenses and the occasional taxi ride to school or some such.

So there we were, fat, dumb and happy. Well, perhaps I should reserve that characterization for myself. Melanie tends to be atop all situations and is seldom in relax mode. Still, all things considered, she appeared settled into the idea of becoming a mother and was now on her fourth child-rearing text. If our daughter emerged from childhood dazed and confused it was likely going to be my fault. Melanie was attempting to ensure at least one adult in the family was prepared for any eventuality.

Adopting Ainsley

And then it was the week before Thanksgiving. A Thursday afternoon to be precise. Tiffany was scheduled for her final pre-delivery medical checkup and I was banging away on a paper for one of our Defense Department clients. A little after 2 pm my phone rang. Leaning over to check the caller-ID I saw it was Melanie. Now this was a little unusual. Melanie is typically busy and I normally make the phone calls. Today, she was at a conference with most of her organization's major donors. I wasn't expecting to hear from her or see her until after 10:00 pm. But with Tiffany close to her delivery date, I knew Melanie kept her Blackberry close at all times so thought she might have heard the news that the baby was on the way.

"Hi Dear." Standard opening for what was about to become a very unnerving conversation. "Tiffany went to her regular doctor's appointment and they could not detect a heartbeat." What? "I'm sorry, can you repeat that?" "The doctor could not detect the baby's heart beat." I'm thinking the medical system has simply screwed up...we're only 10 days from delivery and everything has gone fine, Tiffany was young, and taking great care of herself...this must be a mistake. "Has she asked for a second opinion?" Melanie paused. "Yes, they think the baby is dead." Dead? Did I just hear that correctly?

"What, how?" Melanie was also clearly rattled. Her shock came across the phone via the emotionless tone of her voice and her truncated responses to my questions. "We don't know, they are running more tests. I'll call you as soon as they have additional answers." I hung up the line...forgetting to add my standard, "Love You."

Dead? I stared at the computer screen and waved my hands over the keyboard. All productive activity came to a halt. I turned to the window and watched November's cold winds whip the clouds through a grey sky. This was a phone call I was likely never to forget and the weather was doing nothing to brighten my spirits. Rather than sit and ponder my desk, I took to walking the corridors. In a building occupied by intelligence analysts and program managers even this bit of potential mingling can be a lonely affair. Everyone works behind closed doors. The only contact with another human occurred when there was a coincidental urge to visit the restrooms. No solace to be found in aimless wandering.

I walked back into my office, opened the newspaper and pretended to read. What the hell happened? How could a child with a perfectly healthy mother suddenly be dead? Who or what was to blame? I wanted answers…and all I got was silence. No sense in dialing Melanie. I knew she would call as soon as news came from Las Vegas. I diddled away an hour, and then another.

About 4:30 Melanie called. "Tiffany's placenta separated from the uterus. The baby is dead, and may have been dead for a couple of days." So now we had an answer, but the pit in the bottom of my stomach dropped even further. I'm not a doctor, but at moments like this the internet offers lots of explanations. I found the Utah Department of Health web site.

According to the experts, "placental abruption" is the early separation of the placenta from the wall of the uterus. As the placenta provides the growing infant food and oxygen prior to birth, early separation from the uterus "can cause serious problems for the baby and mother." No shit, in this case it was fatal for one member of the equation.

The Utah Department of Health went on to note early separation of the placenta occurs in about one in 120 births. In 20-40 percent of such incidents the separation is fatal for the unborn child. A placental abruption can occur any time after about the 20th week of pregnancy, and takes place more frequently in the last 3 months. (In a normal birth, the placenta does not separate from the uterus until right after the baby is delivered.) Well at least now I understood the medical reason for our would-be daughter's death. But what about the cause…what really happened?

Adopting Ainsley

Utah was less helpful on that front. As the website contritely informed me, you are at a higher risk for placental abruption if you:

- Are a cigarette smoker
- Become pregnant after age 35
- Have had more than 4 or 5 children
- Are pregnant with twins or triplets
- Have high blood pressure
- Use cocaine
- Have diabetes
- Have had a previous abruption
- Have trauma to the uterus such as a car accident

Tiffany fit none of those categories. We were simply the victims of bad luck. I wondered about Tiffany, how must she be doing? This had to be even more devastating for the young lady.

Melanie called back. Tiffany's mother—who had been absent ever since shunting the wayward child off to Nevada—suddenly discovered some empathy for her daughter and was headed for Las Vegas. The doctors were going to induce labor in order to deliver the corpse. I said I was heading home. Melanie said she was leaving the conference and would meet me there. It was a long, quiet night at the Anderson-Sloan residence.

Chapter XIII
If at First You Don't Succeed

By trying we can easily learn to endure adversity—another man's I mean.

—*Mark Twain*

Despite his legion of shortfalls, I still might have something nice to say about Alfred—had he not managed to completely botch the immediate aftermath of our recent tragedy. Oh sure, our attorney called and offered his sympathies. He also reminded us that "these things happen" and then assured us we would be at the top of his list for the next opportunity. Then he proceeded to rapid fire send all the remaining bills for Tiffany and ensure her caretaker in Las Vegas received a full month's payment after the young lady left for home only a week into the current billing period.

Wait, it gets better. Alfred also insisted we should continue to pay for Tiffany's mental health counseling—with his in-house doctor—and that we be prepared to write another check for $5,000 to cover forthcoming adoption expenses. As best I could tell, Alfred either believed we were made of money or that we had a great printing press operating full time in the basement. Neither was true. As the keeper of our accounts, Melanie can attest to same at any time of day or night. I am wise enough to take her word on this…like most men I am checkbook challenged and have little desire to embark on remedial training.

The measure of Melanie's disgust with Alfred became eminently clear on the Wednesday before Thanksgiving. Less than a week after our loss, we were on our way to meet with another adoption attorney—at 08:00 in the morning. I don't know about you, but I have never dealt with a lawyer at 08:00 in the morning. In fact, I used to be fairly certain attorneys did not even appear in their office prior to 8:59. Yes, yes, I've read the John Grisham thrillers that suggest lawyers work endless hours…including sleeping in the office, but I have never been witness to same. In my case—a graduate of the University of Missouri—seeing is believing. I was about to do some seeing.

Harvey Schweitzer had come to Melanie's attention via an acquaintance who offered effusive praise of his dedication and experience. Based in Maryland, Harvey did not offer Alfred's birthmother recruitment skills, but he was plugged into a nation-wide network of fellow adoption specialists…and best yet, appeared willing to show up at meetings both on time and sober. What more could one possibly ask of the man who was potentially going to facilitate the most important decision two adults can make?

So here we were at 07:30 in the morning racing toward an empty office building on the northern edge of Washington DC. That's not fair, the office building was not empty, it simply had no other human beings wandering the halls. A facility designed to house numerous legal and medical professionals, the building was clearly a happening location between 0'ninehundred and 5pm. Outside of those hours it was just another relatively dark collection of corridors and locked doors. Locked doors—I should add—that included the law offices of a one Harvey Schweitzer. Great, another wayward adoption attorney. I was ready to walk out before we even sat down for our first meeting.

Melanie was not going to be so easily defeated. Pulling out her ever-present Blackberry, Melanie hit Harvey's number on the speed dial. We could hear the phone ring…and then be picked up. Someone was actually behind those locked doors. "Hello?" Melanie replied with a polite "Good Morning" and then declared

Adopting Ainsley

we were standing outside Harvey's front door. "Oh, just a minute." Click. Well, he wasn't planning to bill for that conversation, the call lasted less than 15 seconds. (Even the most draconian law firms don't commence billing until you pass the 4 minute mark, or so I am told—my bet, all calls last more than 4 minutes in such cases, but I'm known to be a cynic.)

We kept staring at the door, expecting it to unseal at any second. Instead, an unmarked entrance immediately behind us slowly creaked open. Standing in the door way, a short, balding gentleman who introduced himself as the attorney in question. With little fanfare, Harvey escorted us through the dark office back to a tiny conference room that reeked of old carpet and aging paperwork. "Coffee?" I suspected I was about to be offered yesterday's nuked leftovers…in a Styrofoam cup…nothing worse to do to a coffee snob at that time of day. "Nope, had mine already." Better to pass on the java and proceed right to the meeting.

I'll give Harvey credit; he wasted no time in getting down to business. Rather than discuss the philosophy and virtues of adoption, he explained his role as a facilitator and then identified areas where we could help our cause. Item one, build a brochure explaining why we wanted to adopt and then include pictures that would help a birth mother choose among multiple competing couples. To help illustrate the point, Harvey pulled out a stack of sample self-promotion kits. They ranged from the obviously professional glossy to construction paper hooked together with knitting yarn.

I looked at Melanie, Melanie looked at me, and we both sighed. Alfred had promised these "We're So Cute" brochures were a nicety—not a necessity. Our new attorney was telling us just the opposite. These were a requirement if we wanted to be competitive and adopt sometime in the next 18-24 months. Oh, and by the way, it was best if the brochures appeared to have been manufactured at home. Harvey insisted the Kinko Copies products were out of the question.

It seems birth-mothers like the homemade touch–suggesting the brochure was produced for their eyes only. He also advised us to include lots of pictures and not too much text. "Most birth-mothers are not big readers," he offered, dryly. Suddenly I was contemplating a lot of arts and crafts time in my future…this was clearly not a woodshop project. Ribbons, colored construction paper, and rubber cement. Another deep sigh.

While I was busy snooping through the pile of samples, Melanie was pushing Harvey on offering a list of potential candidates. He could only offer a meager few. One was a mother of four who was serving time for robbery–though she swore she was innocent—while expecting her fifth with a birth father who was an illegal Haitian immigrant…also in jail. The second was undecided, but would make a decision closer to the delivery. The final was four months pregnant and was looking for support until she delivered somewhere in late March 2010. We rapidly ruled out number one—that smelled of trouble coming and going. Number two was out given our experience in Tucson. And number three reminded us of Tiffany—and another pile of bills. Harvey agreed on all points and promised to keep an eye out for future prospects. Meeting adjourned.

Damn, I was impressed. We actually made it in and out of an adoption attorney's office in less than an hour. Alfred had a lot to learn. Melanie asked, "What did you think?" My reply was noncommittal, but positive. "He seems a step up from Alfred, but that's not saying much. That, and I'm not so thrilled about a large cut-and-paste project." Melanie expressed her concurrence with the latter observation and let the former slide. "Still," she offered, "we need to get started on the birth mother letter.

The "we" portion of that final statement worried me. The last time "we" tried to write something as a team—that would be our wedding vows—Melanie landed up rewriting my portion, yes, she rewrote my heartfelt professions of love. Now, I'm no poet laureate,

Adopting Ainsley

but have been known to string at least three coherent sentences together...and I do have a fragile male ego...which suffers brutally every time someone decides to completely toss my submission. I would never make it in the newspaper industry and frequently wonder how I have survived the intelligence community. Trust me; there is no shortage of opinionated editors and supervisors in Spookland.

I chose to swallow my concerns—why start the day in trouble? I could at least wait until after 10am before aggravating my significant other. "Ok Dear, let me pick up construction paper and sort through some pictures. I'll start working the letter this afternoon." That answer sufficed for the moment—so long as I was willing to pick up the right shade of pink for our final product. Hey, don't knock pink...according to Melanie pink is the new black. Another battle not worth having.

I dropped Melanie off at her office and headed home. Nice thing about serving as a national security contractor, I was able to work out of the house most days of the week. Turn on the classical music, fire up the computer, and hit "brew" on the espresso maker. Then came the hard part, imparting words of wisdom on a very unresponsive computer screen. Thank god for a very reliable wireless Internet access and Google. My days of picking through molding books in some dank university library are over. Now when I'm stumped for data or a new idea it takes little more than 30 seconds to be back up and running.

The other delightful part of working at home, no dress code. Now, now...don't get the wrong idea. I'm not a sit around the house in my BVDs kind of guy. Nor am I partial to sweat pants—an atrocious bit of clothing that is typically worn by people who have no intention of sweating...or even exercising. No, I'm a fan of shorts and a fleece, pretty much all year around. I can get away with this attire in the winter because Melanie believes no home should be maintained at a temperature lower than 75. In the summer a fleece is necessary because I have the opposite thought. No home should be allowed to get above 75. Guess you could say we live in a miniature version of Hawaii…at least when it comes to climate control.

Needless to say, this outfit is a real hit with people who meet me walking the dog during a snow storm. It also causes our professional dog walker to periodically shake his head in disbelief. Yes, you read that correctly, we have a professional dog walker. In all honesty, the dog has a lot of staff. She goes to dog day care three days a week and the other two she has someone come and take her for an hour-long stroll. Melanie likes to tell people she got me to fill in the other areas where Cheyenne needed attention. This includes early morning and late-night tours of the neighborhood, brushing, trips to the vet, and the occasional wash. My secret ambition in life is to be treated as well as Melanie's dog…or any woman's dog for that matter.

I used to wonder why women are so nice to their pets—particularly cats and dogs. I mean, women already have men wrapped around their little fingers, why hassle with the furry creatures? Turns out—according to reports I heard on NPR, so it must be true—women feel most strongly about their pets. That's right, pets come before children and even other women friends…and they certainly come before spouses. So the next time a women tells you she treasures you above all others…just keep in mind that your status atop the totem pole can be almost immediately upended by bringing home a puppy or kitten.

Anyway, I went home—donned my favorite pair of paint-stained shorts and commenced to work. Being the Wednesday before Thanksgiving…the government types all were released three hours early…I knocked off the heavy thinking at 2pm and began to mull over the contents of our birth mother letter. How to express sentiments that are indicative of one's morals and values without being preachy or snotty? No simple feat. The nice thing about computers, no wads of paper scattered about the floor after

Adopting Ainsley

being ripped from the typewriter. The down side to computers? No wads of paper to prove you have actually been working on the project your significant other requested this be the all-consuming focus.

Melanie walked in at 6:30 and asked how I was doing on the letter. "Um, I have some draft thoughts." That answer wasn't winning any shouts of joy or pats on the back. "You have draft thoughts?" "Yes dear, but I should be able to get everything in place by the time Monday rolls around." Also a response that drew a less-than laudatory glance.

"How'd you do on finding pictures?" Melanie had me with that question. I didn't even realize I was supposed to be looking for pictures. "Uh, haven't started." So now I've not only managed to not hit a home run…I'm coming close to being thrown out at first base as the result of a poorly executed bunt. Fortunately, on rare occasions I can think fast on my feet. "We can have your mother take some shots over the next couple of days." Melanie's mother is really into photography—and has the equipment necessary to even make me look good. Finally, a right answer. Melanie agreed with this plan and set to work on dinner. I went down to the shop to make saw dust and clear my muddled head.

Believe it or not, even with a house full of guests and the cooking requirements associated with putting on a full Thanksgiving Day spread, we managed to draft a letter and get the pictures necessary for our Anderson-Sloan homemade self-advertisement. We had pictures of Melanie cooking, the two of us sitting together on the back steps, and even a gathering of the entire clan—including the dog. All we needed was 10 copies of each and a lot of rubber cement. As for the letter…well, judge for yourself. A few of my ramblings made the final cut, but as a whole this is a fine bit of Melanie at work. I never wrote letters this well and likely never will.

Eric C Anderson

Dear Birth Mother,

We are Melanie and Eric and we can't wait to be parents.

We live in a sun-filled house in a family friendly neighborhood in Washington DC, that is full of children. There is a beautiful park only two blocks away, which is particularly important to Cheyenne, our super-friendly and much-loved dog.

We are both close to our families and our parents and siblings have been very supportive of our efforts to adopt. Melanie's parents live nearby in Delaware, and her sister Kimberly lives in Philadelphia so we see them both fairly often. Eric's parents and his brother Matthew's family all live in the Seattle area so we talk to them on the phone a lot.

We are warm, outgoing people with lots of close friends. Melanie likes to cook, go to the movies and read novels. Eric likes to work with wood, work out at the gym (Melanie does this, but doesn't enjoy it), ride his motorcycle and spend afternoons in the park with Cheyenne.

We are each other's best friends and we are incredibly lucky to have found each other. Our relationship is based upon open, honest communication, and we are warm and affectionate with one another.

Eric has a son, Sean, from an earlier marriage. Sean is 8 years old and lives in Colorado with his mother. We enjoy seeing him and realized, after having him with us for the summer, how much love we have to share and how much we want to parent a child together.

We have tried to have a child ourselves, but we cannot. We are both very comfortable with adoption; we are absolutely certain we will love an adopted child—of any race—the same as a child born to us. We also want you to know how strongly we value education. There are many terrific schools in our neighborhood and we look forward to becoming active participants in our child's school. We have the resources to make sure he or she can go to college and graduate school.

Melanie is an attorney; Eric is a national security consultant. Melanie has spent her career in public service, while Eric has been in the

Adopting Ainsley

Air Force and taught at a several universities. Melanie has an office in downtown Washington and Eric frequently works from home. The combination works very well for us, and ensures someone is always available to attend school activities and be available for a child's needs at any time of day.

We look forward to sharing child-rearing responsibilities from the very beginning. We believe children need to know both of their parents love them and enjoy spending time with them. We will read to the baby from day 1, knowing that children pick up more than we might think and that reading is such an important skill. Life is about more than just books though, so we will also spend time outdoors at the playground, playing fetch with the dog, and later, playing golf and going sailing (Eric lived on a sailboat for awhile). And because having close friends is so important, we will arrange play dates and encourage the child to play soccer or another team sport. Naturally, we will be at the games to cheer from the sidelines! In addition, Eric thinks that everyone should be handy so he will teach our son or daughter how to change a tire and make basic home repairs. Melanie, on the other hand, thinks everyone should be able to cook so she will teach our son or daughter how to bake cookies and make pasta sauce.

We know how difficult your decision must be and promise that if you choose us to parent your baby, he or she will be raised by loving parents, adoring aunts and uncles and doting grandparents.

Thank you for considering us as adoptive parents. We would be happy to meet you in person or talk on the phone to answer your questions.

Best wishes and good luck with your decision.

Melanie and Eric

See, I told you Melanie is good at putting difficult thoughts into clear English. Must be all that lawyer training. We also managed to mass produce enough photos to assemble 10 of the "love us" brochures. After gluing and sewing....yes, I succumbed to the

Eric C Anderson

pink ribbon for binding pressure…we were ready. A quick trip to Fedex and Harvey was in business…and we were back into searching for a new family member.

Chapter XIV
Close Encounters with Corporate Greed Mongers

The rain...falls upon the just and the unjust alike; a thing which would not happen if I were superintending the rain's affairs. No, I would rain softly and sweetly on the just, but if I caught a sample of the unjust outdoors I would drown him.

—*Mark Twain*

And now we were back to the waiting game. Sort of. In addition to setting up our relationship with Harvey, Melanie also strongly hinted I needed to start looking at "other options." I wisely nodded my head north and south and then headed for my trusty laptop.

I think I've previously noted a search for "adoption" on Google generates somewhere around 98 million hits. A search for "adoption" agency returns 2.5 million options. So how to sort this out?

I didn't know then...and I still don't know now. I tried some obvious options—like picking agencies in adoption-friendly states—but that turned into a fruitless process as many of the organizations would not return my phone calls and others simply declared their existing clients had priority and it could be another 18 months before our name came up on the list. The more calls I made, the grimmer the picture. Melanie would come home for dinner and I had little to offer other than a kiss and a quick return to my woodshop. Sigh.

And then I clicked on the Adoption Network Law Center. The Adoption Network Law Center proclaims it is a "professional law corporation" that provides "quality adoption services to adoptive parents." Sound good, doesn't it? I mean, who wants to deal with unprofessional lawyers who provide half-assed adoption services? Not Melanie or me…one could argue we had already been down that path.

The other draw to the Adoption Network Law Center (ANLC) was the speed at which it claimed to operate. According to a slick brochure they sent me in the mail, "most adopting parents who rely on ANLC's services typically wait no longer than four months after their profile is added to our websites to be selected by a birth-mother." Wow, this is exactly what we had been looking for! How do they accomplish this feat? Again, I'll use their words, "Adoption Network Law Center advertises aggressively via Google, Yahoo! And social networking sites to build relationships nationally with as many birthmothers as possible." They also claim to market in print publications. This appeared to be a real adoption machine.

They also proved to be quite aggressive in pursuing would-be adoptive parents. Less than a week after contacting their offices I had an inch-thick bundle of materials advertising their services, a contract for setting up a legal relationship with the firm, and my very own "adoption consultant." I figured this was "cooking with gas" and would keep me in good stead with Melanie. I was wrong. Not because I had proceeded down an unacceptable path, but because the Adoption Network Law Center was apparently used to dealing with clients who don't read all the fine-print in a contract. That, and they went after us with a "hard-sell" campaign that smelled more of a used-car sale than adoption of a very small person.

Let's start with the contract. I won't bore you with the entirety of a 10 page document that features very tiny font. Instead,

Adopting Ainsley

I'll point out the issues that immediately caught Melanie's legal eye. For openers, the contract declares pre-placement/post-placement and administrative adoptive parents services may include... that's right..."may include," "Communicating all information on significant developments to the adoptive parents." Melanie circled "significant" about four times and scribbled "who decides what is significant?" She was pretty sure it was not the adoptive parents.

It gets worse, trust me. Under a section titled "No Warranty of Birthmother/No Warranty of Health of Child" Melanie discovered the following: "If the baby is born and diagnosed by a medical professional providing care for the child with a serious birth defect or terminal illness, ANLC will attempt to provide the possibility of a presentation of an adoption opportunity to clients at no additional fee other than finalization legal services fees, if applicable." Melanie circled "serious"—same concern as above, who defines "serious"—and then she underlined "will attempt." Her comment, "Very noncommittal and almost certain to blow up in the client's face." And we were only at the top of page three.

Down at the bottom of page five she found this stunner. "If an adoption opportunity rematch is necessary because the clients withdraw from any prospective adoption, for any reason other than the baby is born and diagnosed by a medical professional providing care for the child with a serious birth defect or terminal illness, clients will be responsible for $3,500 as an additional adoption service fee to be paid within seven calendar days of withdrawal, upon which time ANLC will continue to attempt to provide an adoption opportunity to clients." You guessed already. Yes, Melanie again circled the word "serious." She also underlined the cash figure—we were beginning to realize the Adoption Network Law Center was very much a for-profit entity.

You think I'm kidding? Try this item on page six. "If clients decline a birthmother match based on a particular ethnicity or mix thereof, then the clients agree to pay an additional fee of

$6,000 within seven days....If clients fail to timely pay this additional fee, then this agreement shall be terminated at the option of ANLC and all fees paid to ANLC shall be forfeited with no additional obligation on the part of ANLC to clients." Ouch, so far the "penalties" portion of this document was tallying $9,500 and we have yet to discuss initial intake fees or actual placement costs.

But before we get to the question of money, one finds this crowd pleaser at the bottom of page six. "Clients understand that the financial agreements in this contract are confidential and not to be discussed with their birthparent(s). Clients' breach of this confidentiality or any other covenants or conditions of this agreement, clients' default in any financial obligation to ANLC, or clients outward manifestation to terminate clients' relationship with ANLC will give ANLC the right to terminate this agreement along with clients forfeiture of any fees paid to ANLC." What? This agreement is confidential? In my world confidential means that disclosure could endanger national security. I'm pretty sure that was not the case with ANLC's materials...but what do I know? I'm just an intelligence analyst.

The issue of initial cost came up at the bottom of page seven. The privilege of allowing Adoption Network Law Center to assist in our search would cost an immediate $6,800 bucks. Once we sent then the signed contract and cash we would have only 72 hours to rethink the decision—after that "these monies are not recoverable." Melanie underlined that term about six times. She also circled the adoption services fee listed on page eight. That bill came to a nonnegotiable $9,800. See, I told you this was a for-profit business.

The final kicker in this contact came on page nine. In big, bold letters that one could not miss was the following statement. "Clients will keep the terms of this agreement, including but not limited to financial terms and conditions and information concerning ANLC adoption related services, absolutely confidential and will not publicize or disclose such confidential information to anyone." Melanie circled this whole statement and wrote a big question mark in the margin. Neither she nor I could figure out what made this firm's business practices such a state secret.

We were about to learn. Likely aware of the fact this contract and its associated fees could be more than a little off-setting, the Adoption Network Law Center ensured you had a conference call with your "adoption consultant" the night their package arrived in the mail. The woman we landed up talking with was clearly no legal expert, but she was more than willing to stress how rapidly they would be able to link us up with a potential birth mother. In fact, she was more than happy to make that case and repeatedly suggest Melanie discuss her legal concerns with a supervisor at a later date.

We're not done yet. About 20 minutes after our conference call ended the "adoption consultant" was back on the phone hurriedly explaining that they had a Hispanic mother who was three days overdue and was deadly serious about placing what would be her fifth child with adoptive parents. We were also breathlessly informed the father was willing to sign away his rights and…best of all…the doctors were sure the child was a girl. Hmmmm, this all sounded remarkably like exactly the preferences we had outlined in the previous call. The whole trick to closing this deal? We had to have that contract signed and in an overnight pouch—now!

Melanie looked at me, I looked at Melanie, and we both said no. We informed the "adoption consultant" there was no way we could rush into such a decision and would have to sleep on the whole deal. This was not what the voice on the phone wanted to hear, but she was in no position to argue and promised to call again the next evening. Seemed reasonable. We ate supper, Melanie once again reviewed the contract, and then we headed to bed. We had been burned badly enough once, there was no reason to risk a repeat. (I like that old adage, fool me once..shame on you. Fool me twice…shame on me.)

Eric C Anderson

As promised, the following evening our very own "adoption consultant" was back on the phone. The Hispanic woman remained pregnant and not yet in labor. The contract still needed to be signed and a check attached if we were going to have a chance at this option. Melanie answered all this hype with a barrage of legal questions. The "adoption consultant" dodged, weaved, and then finally caved. "Please hold and I will connect you with a supervisor." Click. I could hear the elevator music playing in the background. We had not been disconnected, just placed on hold.

The next participant in the conversation was nowhere near as pleasant as her predecessor. We clearly had the boss on the line, and she was not pleased. Melanie once again began asking her questions about the contact and its multiple penalties. No good answers or explanations, just a curt "That's our procedure." Wrong answer. Melanie went for the jugular—"Please define 'significant,' 'serious' and 'will attempt'." This was not going to be pretty, but I was staying on the phone out of morbid fascination. I've seen Melanie deal with other fools via the telephone—it's never pretty for the other party. Shockingly, this party went to an immediate surrender. "You are simply not intended to by one of our clients. Good luck with your adoption journey. Good bye." Click. No more elevator music, we had been cut off. So much for the Adoption Network Law Center.

I have to admit I never again went shopping for an adoption service via the Internet. Fortunately, I was not alone in my frustration with the experience. Melanie never asked me to repeat the process.

This brought us back to the good old-fashioned attorney in residence approach. By the time Harvey received his stack of handmade adoptive parent brochures, the first week of December had come and gone. The second week slipped by just as quietly. The next thing I knew, we were sitting in Florida hiding from the weather in Washington. Melanie took pains to touch base with Harvey on a regular basis, but the response always came back as "no news." Disappointing to say the least, but not entirely unexpected. Adoption options seemingly drop off in December. It's not that people generally quit having unprotected sex in the March, April, May timeframe (do the math…); instead the holiday factor kicks in. Who wants to contemplate giving a child up for adoption when Santa is hanging out in every mall?

Florida really is a decent place to hide when the dice are not rolling in your favor. The weather in December is generally tolerable. (Oh, it will rain and occasionally drop into the 50s, but that's nothing to whine about when Washington is shivering at 25 and threatening to snarl traffic with a dusting of snow.) The swimming pools tend to be heated and, on really good days, you can even go to the beach. Now I'll admit to being a bit of a beach snob—five years of living in Hawaii will do that to a person—and I'm not much of a fan when it comes to the Atlantic Ocean…too damn cold. All that said, as a social voyeur I have nothing but praise for South Beach. The people watching on South Beach is nothing short of amazing.

Think of it this way. South Beach draws the beautiful people…who occasionally opt to wear very tiny swimsuits, the not-so beautiful people…who, unfortunately, also frequently wear similarly tiny swimsuits, and the downright bizarre. What better way to pass a lazy vacation day? Set up the umbrella about 10:30. At 1 o'clock wander over to the News Café for a late lunch and glass of pinot. Stroll back out to your book for a couple more hours of sun and then head for home; preferably no later than 4.

This last bit of advice is not to be ignored. Florida has many virtues—the driving talents of local residents is not one of them. As Dave Barry, the humorist, once observed, drivers in Florida all follow the rules of the road from their native country. This means one can drive 30mph regardless of the expressway lane you occupy. Florida drivers remind me why Melanie controls the keys a majority of the time…I would go insane having to weave through the standard disaster.

My complaints about driving in Florida reflect the fact we have to commute to South Beach from Aventura—the urban area formally known as North Miami. Aventura, like much of the greater Miami urban sprawl, is a collection of high rise condos and asphalt parking lots. Relatively unremarkable, except that Aventura also is home to one of Florida's largest and most successful malls and happens to be the location of a condo Melanie's grandparents purchased back in the 1970s. The grandparents died years ago, but the condo remains in the family. The dwelling comes with a couple of swimming pools, good parking, and is right on the Intercoastal Waterway…no hotel fees. Good deal made even better by the nearby delis specializing in fresh bagels and hand carved lox. Suffice it to say we try to migrate down to Florida for two weeks in December and every long weekend between then and the end of March.

Alas, December and January pass with no development on the adoption front. Melanie periodically noted this fact, and I quietly concurred and spent more time in the woodshop. No sense in picking a scab that neither of us can make heal. Harvey, meanwhile, claimed to be advocating and circulating for our cause. I knew this because Melanie would mention a phone call or bill from our attorney—and then change the topic.

Oh, in the midst of our moping one of our friends with children decided to chime in with some parental advice. "Go live it up now." That's right, we were being told to go whoop it up…to stay out late…party in Paris…in short, do all those fun things adults are supposedly entitled to enjoy. The reasoning for this advice, once we had a small being in the house the fun meter would be essentially turned off. Huh, not exactly what prospective parents want to hear. I was willing to immediately heed this bit of wisdom,

Adopting Ainsley

until Melanie reminded me that we didn't exactly live a hedonist lifestyle even without children. Given our schedules, we were usually in bed by 10:30 and our nights out tended more toward dinner and a movie rather than late night clubbing or bar-hopping.

We did have the occasional trip to someplace nice—Paris for a long weekend in May the previous year—but on a routine basis we pretty much lived the lifestyle of the old people we had become. While my teeth were not resting in a glass by the bed yet, she did have a point, we were not the wild party animals DINKs (Dual Income, No Kids) are assumed to be. We already lived like people with children; the big difference as best we could tell was an absence of diapers and an absolute lack of milk in the refrigerator. Making lemonade of lemons we mutually agreed this would at least make the transition to small person world would less jarring than people were telling us. The cynics are wrong, in some cases ignorance is bliss.

Chapter XV
From Corporate Greed to Shady Characters

A sin takes on a new and real terror when there seems a chance that it is going to be found out.

—*Mark Twain*

I don't know if Harvey ever heard about our run-in with the Adoption Network Law Center. Somehow I suspect we never thought it was worth further conversation. We did, however, take great pains to warn other would-be adoptive parents about snakes in the corporate grass. Hey, if people can give us advice about how to go out and live it up, the least we can do is return the favor by offering similar free wisdom to other human beings. Typically, people tend to ignore such observations when they come from me—they are much more prone to listen when Melanie speaks. Something about credibility and a proven track record. I work in intelligence—the only career field that is allowed to be wrong more often than the weather guessers—Melanie is in a serious business...keeping politicians in line.

By late January, I was beginning to think we needed more unethical politicians. The lack of news from Harvey was really getting to Melanie. In an effort to avoid pouring gasoline on a fire, I stopped asking if she had heard from our attorney and instead focused on safer conversations—like how cold Washington could be in the winter. No debate there, but it makes for a dull dinner conversation...particularly when you are on iteration five of the same subject. I thought about engaging in talks on China and economics—areas I find endlessly interesting—Melanie suggested that would be akin to her discussing the latest soap opera developments. So we agreed to go on mumbling about the temperature and both silently stewed about the status of our would-be little person.

And then, like a bolt out of the blue, it happened. Harvey called to declare he had a potential candidate. A young lady located in Florida who was due to deliver sometime in March. Talk about the best of all possible worlds. Florida is an adoption-friendly state and March was just a short six weeks away. Making things even better, Laura—the mother to be—lived in Fort Lauderdale, a very short trip from the condo in Aventura. You may recall we needed the blessing of the Inter-state Compact folks before the baby could be trundled off to Washington. Now, instead of living in a hotel room, we could actually plan on staying in a familiar place with all the trappings of home…plus a swimming pool. It don't get much better than this. Well it does, but we're talking about children here…not cigars, old whiskey and fast motorcycles.

Doing his best to keep us informed, Harvey immediately emailed the young lady's intake form. This is the document a birthmother must fill out so that the attorneys can begin the process of locating potential adoptive parents. I had only seen one of these over the course of our adventure—the document Tiffany had completed—and so was poorly prepared for the disaster that scrolled down my computer screen. If you thought Tiffany came from a tough family, you ain't seen nothing yet.

Laura was 18, single, white and nominally Catholic. The birth father was 22, single, and also white. Nothing worrisome so far…. now steel yourself for a trip into American unhappiness. Laura, who was morbidly obese, declared the birth father had initially told her to get an abortion because he already had two children and didn't want a third. In her barely legible scribble, she went on to declare "We don't have a relation becuz (sic) he's with his baby-mother and his kids. Verbally abusive." Not too hard to picture this "winner" sitting out front a rusting mobile home dressed in a dirty wife-beater tank top, cold beer in hand...at about 9 in the morning.

It gets worse. When asked to describe her family, Laura offered the following observations. Mom was an administrative assistant with a "votech" education who enjoyed bicycling, swimming and yoga. Her father had no job and no education, but did engage in the hobbies of "drugs and drinking." Laura's two brothers sounded slightly more stable–at least they were employed. At ages 23 and 20, they were a cashier and "meat man," respectively. Neither had an education worthy of listing and their hobbies were "fishing" and "cars." A younger sister—age 15—was still in school and—in a sign of some hope—had an interest in computers. All told, however, it didn't seem like this group would be retiring to the Riviera anytime soon.

Laura seemed to understand her family situation was perilous as she indicated she wanted to place the child for adoption because, "I'm not ready for a child and have no education. I would like for my child to have a better life than me." Melanie teared up when she read this statement. I was too busy searching for the medical background data to get emotional. If there was one thing that could derail this adoption prospect it would be drug usage. Given the statements above, and Laura's socio-economic status, I was more than just a little worried we were going to be reading about a heavy crystal meth addiction.

While the effects of methamphetamine addiction in adults are fairly well known, much less work has been done on meth and unborn children. According to a study published in the *American Family Physician,* "Although methamphetamine crosses the placenta, data regarding in utero effects are limited. Placental insufficiency and abruption can occur, and maternal deaths have been reported. Fetal effects reported include intrauterine growth retardation, prematurity, clefting, cardiac anomalies, and death."

And what happens if the child actually survives the pregnancy? The study's authors were no more reassuring on that front. "There are few data regarding methamphetamine exposure in children. Withdrawal from stimulant exposure is usually milder than opiate withdrawal in neonates, but abnormal sleep patterns, poor feeding, tremors, and hypertonia have been reported. One study found that 49 percent of neonates exposed to methamphetamine exhibited such withdrawal signs, although only 4 percent required medication." In other words, the child tends to go through withdrawal, thereby starting a new life even more miserably for both baby and would-be parents.

We're not done. Here's all science knows about the lingering after-effects of mother's meth use. "Long-term effects of prenatal methamphetamine exposure are unclear. A 14-year follow-up study of children born to women who abused amphetamines in pregnancy showed academic and mild physical delays, but there were many potential confounders."[1] Just my guess, but the "many potential confounders" statement is a fancy way of saying the children were probably not growing up in a home that placed much emphasis on education, exercise, or anything that looked like a traditional family environment. This makes it hard to sort out the difference between birth defects and just plain poor parenting. Not that it matters, I was unwilling to experiment with a child who started life way behind the power curve because mom wanted to be high all the time.

Melanie, by the way, likes to remind me this attitude about meth may be unfounded. An avid *New York Times* reader, she frequently cites reporting on how the supposedly condemned generation of "crack babies" has actually emerged from the scourge relatively unscathed. Seems she's on the mark. A professor of psychiatry at Brown University has found no statistically significant effect on these crack exposed children's I.Q. or language development. (One study of crack babies revealed the I.Q. scores of exposed children only averaged about 4 points lower at age 7 than those of unexposed children.)

This is not to say all is well with the crack babies. "In tests that measure specific brain functions, there is evidence that cocaine-exposed children are more likely than others to have difficulty with tasks that require visual attention and "executive function"—the brain's ability to set priorities and pay selective attention, enabling the child to focus on the task at hand. Cocaine exposure may also increase the frequency of defiant behavior and poor conduct. There is also some evidence that boys may be more vulnerable than girls to behavior problems."[2]

Any way you look at it, drug use by pregnant women is simply a bad thing for the infant. I realize I'm not the first rocket scientist to reach this conclusion, and I didn't want to cast aside a seemingly viable adoption opportunity simply because the young lady's background suggested a sizable potential for meth abuse. This left one option, read through the medical background information Harvey had included in his email.

Not surprisingly, the first two pages of medical information Laura was asked to provide specifically focused on medication/drug use. The first page—including the block for amphetamines—was all checked no. Whew. Page two was less reassuring. In the block for marijuana use Laura had checked yes, declared this occurred during the second month of her pregnancy, and then made this statement in the "type, frequency and amount" column: "not sure." Not sure? What the hell did that mean? She was unsure of the type? The frequency? Or the amount? Sigh. At least pot was not crystal meth or crack.

In fact, the Merck Online Medical Library offers this comment on pot and pregnancy, "Marijuana: Whether use of marijuana during pregnancy can harm the fetus is unclear. The main component of marijuana, tetrahydrocannabinol, can cross the placenta and thus may affect the fetus. However, marijuana does not appear to increase the risk of birth defects or to slow the growth of the fetus. Marijuana does not cause behavioral problems in the newborn unless it is used heavily during pregnancy." As best I could tell, even if Laura was a complete stoner the worst we could suffer is a child with the munchies. I chuckled at this observation. Melanie didn't think I was so funny. She did, however, agree with my recommendation that we tell Harvey to proceed with establishment of a formal legal relationship. We were back on track.

Sort of. Harvey's legal counterpart in Florida was a one Mike Lost. Mike was the sole proprietor of Adoptions, Incorporated, and seemed to specialize in finding young women who came from the proverbial wrong side of the tracks. As we shall shortly see, I have reasons for coming to this conclusion. Trust me; this is not middle class snobbishness or a judgment statement. Mike knew the seedy side of society as well as I know confines of my workshop. The other thing about Mike, he had the thickest Russian accent I have ever heard coming from an American attorney.

First things first. Before any progress could be made money was going to have to change hands. Mike demanded we immediately wire him $9,000 so he could commence filling out documents and making sure Laura was receiving proper medical care. He mumbled something about the funds being non-refundable, but also assured us that Laura was "100% in the adoption corner." Boxing analogies from a Russian-American adoption lawyer? Egad.

As had been the case with Tiffany, Melanie was adamant the issue of father's rights be addressed as soon as possible. Mike gave us a "no worries" response and then dropped off the radar scope for almost five days. This type of behavior was, well, less than "no worries" on our side of the phone line. In her original paperwork Laura had declared she did not know where the birth father was located. Harvey assured us, however, that he had done business with Mike in the past and there was nothing to worry about. Easy

Adopting Ainsley

for him to say. We were now staring at a calendar that was rapidly headed for March and were down another $9,000. "No worries" my ass.

About 5pm on the fifth day Mike resurfaced. Seems the issue of father's rights was a little more complicated than we had been led to believe. As it turns out, Laura's ex-boyfriend was on the run from the law. (Ah, my comment on wife-beater tank top and a rusting mobile home was closer to the mark than even I suspected.) Nonetheless, Mike had managed to hunt him down and was now in possession of the appropriately signed legal documents. Think about this for a minute, the adoption attorney managed to locate a wanted criminal and then convince the thug to sign formal documents. Mike was either very connected with shady characters or was a very large person. Or perhaps both were true. I don't know, we never actually met the man.

Not for the want of trying. In mid-February, Melanie had us slated for a three-day weekend in Florida. She passed this data along to Harvey and Mike…stating it might be a great opportunity for us to meet with Laura. The two attorneys thought this would be a good idea, the young lady said she was willing, and so we penciled in a face-to-face session on the final day of our stay. This decision was purposeful. Laura had stated Saturday and Sunday were out….this left Monday. We were in no position to argue. Monday it was.

Just let me say these initial meetings with birthmothers never get easier. By the time Monday rolled around Melanie and I were worrying about the coming meet and greet. Having gone through two very unpleasant experiences and subsequently been placed on hold for months, we wanted nothing more than to have Laura find us suitable parents. We purchased a small gift, I dressed in something that appeared responsible, and then we waited for the phone to ring. According to the plan, Mike would call with a meeting on Monday morning. By 11:30 it was clear he either lacked a watch or something was amiss with the pregnant 18-year old. At 11:45 Melanie called Mike. No answer. That prompted a call to Harvey. No answer.

At 1 o'clock Mike finally returned the favor. He explained he could not get in touch with Laura, and so was going to have to cancel. If Melanie could have laid hands on Mike at that point all bets would have been off. "Could not get in touch?" Mike stammered a "no" into the phone and then began employing evasive maneuvers. Melanie was not letting this one go. "You couldn't stop by and speak with her?" Mike had no answer. "What are we paying you for?" Now there was a question I would have liked to hear him answer. Mike was wise enough not to try. Even a lousy lawyer apparently knows when silence is the best course of action.

Melanie hung up and commented as we walked out to the pool. "I'm getting a bad feeling about this whole arrangement." As I've said before, Melanie is a professional worrier, so these words didn't surprise me. I countered with a bit of optimism—"We are not dealing with America's finest, maybe she just panicked." Wrong choice of terms. "If she panics about a meeting, how is she going to agree to on the adoption?" Melanie had me on this one. She was right. If the young lady was too nervous to meet with us informally, how was she going to be willing to relinquish a very small child? Now I was feeling blue as well.

We flew home early Tuesday morning still unsure of future. Washington in February is absolutely depressing. The days are short, the grass is brown, the trees naked, and the temperatures hover in the low 30s. The only member of the family who seemingly approves of these conditions is the dog…and even she spends little time hanging around outside. Unless it snows, then the dog is a proverbial pig in the mud. She buries her nose in the frosty white stuff and rolls around in it until we have a large white version of what used to be our brown and gray canine. While the dog likes the white stuff, I am completely dismayed. No motorcycle time until the streets clear. Yup, Washington in February is miserable. And it was about to get worse.

Less than a week after our failed meeting with Laura, Harvey called Melanie at work. "Laura just delivered her baby." Huh? Seems the young lady had suddenly gone into labor and had given birth at the 36 week mark. Harvey informed Melanie that mother and daughter were fine, but…take a deep breath, you know where this is going…but, "Laura has decided to keep the child." Melanie asked Harvey to pass along our congratulations and statement to the effect of "we understand and respect your decision." What else could we say?

Melanie then asked about the $9,000 we had passed along to Mike. Harvey had no answers on that issue. Our attorney did promise to look into the matter and then hung up the phone. He would "look into the matter?" How about a commitment to aggressively pursue a return of most of our hard-earned cash? I didn't need to ask Melanie if she had pushed Harvey on the money. I knew she had. For the moment it felt as though we had just been robbed of $5,000. In fact, we kind of wondered if there actually was a Laura…or if the whole thing had been concocted over vodka in Mike's office.

Harvey assured us Mike was a straight shooter and that he would not engage in such a fraud. Something about "ruining his good name." Pardon me, but Mike was now in the same category as Alfred—a private adoption attorney who graduated in the bottom half of his less than stellar law school. I was livid and made that clear to Harvey in no uncertain terms. Intent on keeping us as clients, a wise move given the amount of billing he was racking up in our name, Harvey stated he would contact Mike and seek redress. I, for one, was not holding my breath, but agreed to let him try.

The best Harvey could do? Mike called us to declare he would continue seeking a potential birth mother and that we were at the top of his list for prospective parents. News of this "wondrous" development caused me to quit holding my breath permanently. If Mike was anything, he was undependable. And now we were going to place all our eggs in that very questionable basket? No, but it was another possible lead—and lord knows Mike was also looking forward to the possibility of sending us more bills in the future. We reluctantly agreed to this plan, asked Harvey to keep his eyes open for other options, and went back to talking about the weather. February was turning into the longest month on the calendar.

Oh, by the way, if you ever wondered how attorneys deal with other way-ward attorneys…here's Melanie's letter to Mike on the whole issue…guess what, in the end he sent back $4,500. Not impressive on his behalf, but very revealing about Melanie's ability to use the English language. Oh, by the way, steel yourself, this letter lays out in black and white all the various issues adopting parents can confront—from poor accounting, to manipulative birthmothers, and, finally, potentially less than scrupulous lawyers.

Melanie Sloan
March 18, 2009

Dear Mr. Lost:

My husband, Eric Anderson, and I request that you return a significant portion of the $9,000 we paid you on February 4, 2009 to facilitate the adoption of a baby your client, Laura, was then expecting.

As you know, Eric and I signed a contract in regard to this adoption and emailed it to you on February 3, 2009. The following day, we wired $9,000 to you because you would not accept a check, the more typical practice of lawyers.

After you received our money and the signed contract, we attempted to schedule a meeting with the birth mother during a planned trip to Florida, February 12-17. After receiving no response from you to that request, finally on Sunday evening February 15, our lawyer, Harvey Schweitzer, informed us we were to meet Laura the next morning,

Adopting Ainsley

February 16, at either 9:30 or 10:00 am, with the exact location to be determined in the morning. After 10:00 am passed and we heard nothing about the meeting, we called Mr. Schweitzer who said he would try to get in touch with you.

Distressed by these events, the afternoon of the 16th, I sent Mr. Schweitzer an email stating that I was beginning to be concerned that we had been the victims of a fraud. I wrote:

Does whatever happened today suggest there is a problem with this adoption? We are worried that we wired Mike $9,000 (when most lawyers accept checks), never received a receipt for the funds or a signed contract, and that a meeting was vaguely scheduled at the very last minute with no details, leaving us waiting all morning and then we heard absolutely nothing as to why there was no meeting after all. On top of that, I know you have had trouble reaching Mike recently. If you had not had a long history with this lawyer, I might think we could be the victims of some sort of scam.

Mr. Schweitzer replied:

I just spoke to Mike. It is his fault there was no meeting. He is going to Laura's home tomorrow morning. He could not reach her yesterday or today. He had told her last month when you would be back. She wanted the meeting. Mike got really busy last week and waited till Sunday to call her w/ the time/place. He could not reach her. In the past he has always been able to reach her quickly. He will sign the contract and send it back ASAP.

We heard nothing further until I emailed Mr. Schweitzer on February 23rd, stating:

We never got the signed contract back and have had no updates. Have you heard any news from Mike? Did Laura decide she did not want to speak to us on the phone after all? I have to be in FL on business Wed. through Friday of next week. If it is necessary, I could meet Laura sometime during that period. We are feeling pretty uncertain about the status of the adoption. Do you think it is still on or should we be looking for other options?

Late on the afternoon of the 23rd, I finally received the signed contract. Remarkably, the very next morning Mr. Schweitzer called to inform me that the baby had been born and Laura had decided to keep her. He also forwarded me an email he had received from you:

Heard from Laura late yesterday. She delivered by emergency the other day, at 36 weeks but she is keeping the baby. According to what the doctors told her the baby's size was 34 weeks along and stopped growing about 2 weeks ago. The baby is in the NICU; she doesn't know when the baby will be going home.

The adoptive parents will get $1700.00 back because I didn't pay Laura's March expenses from the money they wired. I will overnight the money to you tomorrow for delivery on Thursday.

Less than 30 minutes later, Mr. Schweitzer sent me another email:

I had a talk with Mike just now. He wants to do his best for you and try to reduce any financial loss. He and I will talk later today and I will also have an e-mail from him. As of right now do not assume that all the money (minus the $1700) is a loss.

I responded that afternoon:

Eric and I are particularly concerned about the fact that Mike is willing to return only $1700 to us. First, we wired that money a mere three weeks ago and to be charged $7300 for this brief period seems excessive. In addition, we were told that $4,000 was to support Laura, meaning at the very minimum we would be due $2500 (for the 3 out of 8 weeks we actually signed on to support her). Further, Mike's $5,000 fee for his role in this fiasco seems unjustified.

Second, Mike apparently only signed the contract with us in the last couple of days, likely after Laura gave birth, suggesting we had no contract with him.

Third, as you can see from my emails over time, I have been suspicious of the circumstances surrounding this potential adoption. It was odd that though you informed Mike we would be in Florida the weekend of Feb. 13th back in late January, and then emailed him again shortly before our trip, he never made any effort to reach out to Laura to see if she wanted to meet us. His "scheduling" a meeting for the morning of Monday the 16th when he had never conferred with Laura about such a meeting was further suspect. To top it off, Eric and I were left waiting the entire day unclear as to whether or not we were to meet this young woman, when Mike knew he had never actually scheduled the meeting was outrageous. It appears that only because I contacted you yesterday to let you know I would be returning to Florida and you reached out to Mike last night that you were informed the young woman had given birth and decided to keep the baby.

As you will recall, I have previously suggested that it seemed as if Eric and I had been the victims of some sort of scam and it appears that we have been. Obviously, we have no way of knowing if Mike was involved in unethical activity, but I cannot help but wonder if you were told the real reason that the first adoption broke down and if Laura ever actually intended to place the baby for adoption or if she just wanted further financial support during her pregnancy.

I will look forward to hearing your thoughts on all of this.

Since the 24th, we have received no further correspondence pertaining to that adoption situation or a refund of any portion of the $9,000.

First, because it appears that Laura had given birth to the baby before we ever received the signed contract, there may not have been a valid contract in the first place. As an attorney, you may bill us at an hourly rate for the time you spent on this adoption, but I expect to see a bill accounting for your time and activities in relation to this matter. It seems unlikely that such activities would have resulted in a fee of $5,000 so you must return to us any unused portion of the $9,000 we wired to you on February 4th.

Second, under Florida bar rule 5-1.1, money entrusted to an attorney for a specific purpose, including advances for fees, costs, and expenses, is held in trust and must be applied only to that purpose. A refusal to account for and deliver over such property upon demand shall be deemed a conversion. By retaining money intended for use to support Laura during the course of her pregnancy, but never spent for that purpose, you may be in violation of rule 5-1.1.

Notably, given that another family had previously planned to adopt Laura's baby, that all support for a birth mother is typically paid into a trust account at the time adoptive parents agree to the prospective adoption, and that such funds are not returnable if adoptive parents decide against proceeding with the adoption, it seems likely the earlier adoptive parents had covered Laura's costs for the duration of her pregnancy and that we were being billed for costs already covered. Thus, it seems Eric and I may be owed the entire $4,000 we sent you for Laura's expenses. In any event, however, by your own admission you did not use our funds to pay Laura's March expenses and there can be no question that at a bare minimum we are owed those funds. We expect a detailed accounting of any money spent on Laura.

In addition, before we had agreed to the adoption we had been informed Laura's expenses were $2,000 per month, not $1,700 per month, the amount you expressed willingness to return in your February 24th email. As you claimed your fees were $5,000 and if Laura's upkeep was $3,400 for two months, $600 of the $9,000 we sent you remains unaccounted for and this must be returned to us.

In sum, this has been a very unpleasant experience for my husband and me and we would like to wrap it up as quickly as possible. To that end, I expect to receive an immediate and thorough accounting of the $9,000 we entrusted to you as well as a refund of a significant portion of that money. I hope we can resolve this matter amicably, without further action on our part. I look forward to your prompt reply.

Sincerely,

Melanie Sloan, Esq.

cc: Harvey Schweitzer, Esq.

Case closed.

Chapter XVI
If at First (or Second) You Don't Succeed...

Perseverance is a principle that should be commendable in those who have judgment to govern it.

—*Mark Twain*

Yes, yes, I realize February is not the longest month on the calendar, that was just a means of emphasizing the level of frustration we were experiencing in the world of private adoption. As Melanie began to periodically remind me, we should have gone with the agency facilitating Ethiopian adoptions…by now we might have a child in our house rather than just a spare bedroom with a crib. She had a point, but I liked to counter with the argument that we might also still be doing the paperwork required to satisfy a court in Addis Ababa. A court, I might add, that closes for the monsoon season and really sees no reason to rush through documents forwarded from some crazy foreigner who clearly has too much money.

Melanie took all my silliness about rain storms and court systems in stride. As it turns out, she was already seeking back up options—adoption attorney number three. After Mike's shenanigans, Melanie was ready to wash her hands of Harvey. Climbing into her endless list of contacts and business cards, Melanie found a trusted advisor who might be able to help. The result, Robert… the hard-headed lawyer in Florida who had facilitated Supreme Court Justice Robert's adoption of a small person. Talk about a hard-to-dispute credential. If there was someone who should be able to spot a worthless attorney, it had to be the Chief Justice of all these United States.

The trick to Robert: he only took referred clients and he had a reputation for being very difficult to work with. Perhaps it would be more accurate to say, it was Robert's way or the highway. Fine with me, so long as he delivered the goods and put an end to our adoption odyssey. Melanie was of a similar opinion, but went on to warn me that Robert was not cheap—for the privilege of putting up with his nitpicking and badgering we would have to shell over something in the vicinity of $50,000. My hopes of ever owning that Audi A-8 evaporated in a vision of legal bills and stinky diapers. Ah well, probably couldn't afford the insurance and maintenance costs anyway. But still, $50,000? This guy better be good.

I should have known better than to use my outside voice when expressing such reservations. Melanie gave me a funny look and then rhetorically asked, "What about handling Justice Robert's adoption didn't you hear?" Damn, I have got to get a better grasp on what comes out of my mouth. The demons wandering about my enfeebled mind were causing endless grief when exposed to daylight. "I'm sorry dear, was just thinking about the cost. Let's go ahead in seeking a referral."

Demonstrating her usual "I planned this trip before leaving the house" competence, Melanie informed me she already had someone in mind for making the call to Robert. Her referrer was willing to make the introduction, but again warned Robert could be prickly and was not an attorney for everyone. Melanie had made clear we understood that to be the case, and then highlighted the fact we were willing to deal with the personality issues so long as the result was a successful adoption. Apparently the answers was to the positive, because Robert called Melanie at her office a few days later and said he would be willing to take on our case. Whew.

Adopting Ainsley

At about the same time Melanie was working through our attorney issues, I received notification that it was time for my periodic security clearance polygraph. One of the joys associated with working in the intelligence community is a trip to the polygraphist. These folks are the dentists of the classified world. No one likes to go see them, they seem to favor stuffy offices with uncomfortable furniture, and they always find something that needs further examination. The flip side, like the tooth doctor they can serve a valuable function—in this case, deterring espionage. Or so we are told. I remain skeptical. My bosses are not, so off to the polygraph world I go.

For me this means an hour long trip to a facility in the vicinity of Dulles Airport. Typically this is a great excuse for a motorcycle ride...even when the temperature is hovering somewhere to the south off freezing. To keep warm, I simply put on leathers (chaps, jacket, gloves), pull the helmet over my ears, and light a cigar. One tends to arrive a bit chilled...more on that in a moment...but the shivering is worth the airing out prior to being asked to lie about mundane things like your name. I'm not kidding—how else do you validate the test of truth or fiction?

Oh, before I forget, my other bit of preparation is a heady dose of Warren Zevon and Hunter S. Thompson. Warren Zevon, an acquired taste, is the musician responsible for "Werewolves of London" and fare like "Lawyers, Guns & Money" and "Mr Bad Example." Warren's sardonic perspective helps shape my attitude—cynicism is, I believe, the phrase best used in this case. Hunter, on the other hand, assists in framing my answers. Think of it this way, Hunter practiced "gonzo journalism"...an art that often made it difficult to distinguish where truth left off and fiction took over. A perfect approach when responding to people who are paid to doubt everything you say.

So I show up for the poly at my directed 08:00 appointment with a warped mind, dressed in leather, reeking of cigar smoke, and suffering very, very cold hands. At 08:15 the interrogator of the day comes down and yanks me out of the lounge—I am spared more Fox "news," but do not look forward to the substitute...a modern variant of the Spanish Inquisition. After a bit of small talk we get down to business. This means strapping on a device to measure breathing, a heart monitor, and a device purported to measure the sweatiness of one's hands. Some of you can already see where this is going.

Over the course of about an hour I am asked questions about my honesty, loyalty, and lifestyle choices. The latter I find particularly annoying, as I have informed the man behind the machine that we have just completed the process of getting cleared for an adoption—the government knows more about me from that ordeal than they learned during my last security investigation. He is not impressed. "I keep getting bad readings, particularly from your hand." I innocently ask, "What kind of bad readings?" To wit he responds, "I get no readings, it's like your fingers are frozen."

"Well," respond, "in all honesty they probably are...I rode a motorcycle out here." Now the poly guy is no longer looking at me as potential spy, I'm pretty sure he thinks I'm crazy. "You rode out here when it's 25 degrees outside?" Not really a question, but since we're no longer playing stump the chump or catch the spook I feel free to answer. "Of course, the sun was out and the roads are dry. I have my wife's complete blessing." Well, the last part is a lie, but the counterintelligence folks don't really care about how Melanie judges my relatively benign insanity.

The poly bubba stands up, walks out, and lets the door slam behind him. Sigh, looks like I'll be here longer. This waiting thing is part of the game. They ask you questions, go away to "read the results" and then come back to see if you will offer different responses. Oh, and they watch you through a camera to see if you are visibly stewing while the witch doctor is out of the room. My solution to this boring act, read the newspaper...a behavior not

Adopting Ainsley

entirely accepted, but not prohibited either. Like I said, this whole thing is a carefully choreographed dance.

The difference is that this time the polygraph administrator is back within two minutes bearing a heated pad to thaw my digits. Seems I am not the only one who shows up with ice in the veins. I thank him for the unexpected kindness and we get back to the task—truth or consequences. I lose and get the consequences, a return visit. Not to worry, this is a common fate. I have been in the intelligence community for over 20 years and have yet to meet someone who passed on the first round. We always get to come back for more. I suspect this is job security for the poly folks—security argues quite the contrary, they are protecting our nation from would-be bad guys.

Enough of my woes, back to the story at hand. Having lined up a replacement for Harvey, and not seeing much hope for progress on the adoption front in the near future, Melanie suggested it was time we consider a vacation. We're talking a serious vacation—like hours on a plane, dealing with people who don't speak the same language, exotic locales—you know, something akin to visiting Texas. Actually, Texas was out. Aside from Austin, Melanie could find little reason for entering Lyndon Johnson's "hallowed grounds." Nope, we're talking about leaving the U.S. for other parts of the planet. Cool.

We had put our lives on hold for the past year or so with the view that we could have a baby any day. Our time and money had all been adoption focused. Once Laura fell through, Melanie decided it was time to stop thinking about what might be and focus more on the here and now. She also wanted to get away from the anxiety that the last 12 months had wrought. We were expecting a decent tax refund and Melanie wanted to spend it travelling somewhere far away.

The tricky part was where to go. As Melanie is not a big fan of flying, she would like to keep the plane time below 8 hours. I, on the other hand, could care less about the flight, but don't want to land up where there are no gyms or ready access to a drink with dinner. Last time, the compromise was Paris (if the City of Lights can ever really be a compromise), Melanie's favorite city. The food is good, she speaks the language, and I get to indulge in the Louvre and long walks along the Seine. I would note there's a marked shortage of weight rooms in Paris—the French apparently see little need for such silly expenditure on one's energy—but nothing I can't resolve by doing a lot of pushups and sit-ups.

Having ruled out Paris by virtue of the fact we were there less than 9 months ago, other options are laid on the table. Melanie's next choice is always Africa. Not an 8 hour flight, but she has long said she would willingly suck up the airline time for the possibility of seeing really cool animals. She wants to see South Africa and then go on a safari. I'm game for the first portion of this proposed escapade, but could care less about the second. I find staring at animals as they snarf down weeds or wade in murky water a less than thrilling adventure. Furthermore, that safari thing inevitably involves wandering about on the ground where lions and tigers roam free. Why, pray tell, do I want to go be a tourist where I am on a lower rung of the food chain? Despite the inherent logic, this argument never works…the only thing that saves me from Africa is money. A trip like the one Melanie envisions will require me to take a third job.

So we go to considering other possibilities. I suggest Australia. "Too much flying." China. "Too crowded and the food is unappealing." Japan. "Raw fish…nope." Canada. "Too cold." Argentina. "Hmmmmmmm." I've always wanted to go to Argentina. The scenery is said to be spectacular, the food unparalleled, and the wine country worth every moment of your time. Better yet, if we headed for Argentina in the late March timeframe spring would be in the air south of the equator. This meant we would avoid the discomfort of baking or freezing that can make tourism a less than pleasurable experience.

We both realized that going to Argentina meant a tour that will largely cover the place from north to south, east to west. We're talking a lot of flying and dodging through traffic. Why? Well, the Iguazu Falls are at Argentina's Northern extreme, Patagonia at the southern end, Mendoza—wine country—on the western border, and Buenos Aries is on the eastern coast. Like I said, a lot of flying and scurrying about. But hey, if you're only going someplace once in your life, make it worth the trip.

Melanie assigned me the duty of finding a travel agent—too hard to line all these venues up by one's self—and she went back to engaging with Robert. It seems Robert was insistent that we have all our legal ducks in a row before setting up a meeting in his offices, meaning he wanted to be sure we had a home study done and we were ready to take on a child. This was not a case of Robert being anal retentive, rather it reflected the fact he was often able to match a birthmother with prospective parents in a very short period of time. He didn't want to be standing around waiting for us to dot the i's and cross the t's. He was also insistent we be very clear in the type of birthmothers we were willing to meet. Melanie made clear we were not interested in supporting someone for an extended period. Instead, she filled Robert in on our recent history and told him we preferred a birthmother who was about to deliver. Melanie also made sure Robert knew we were not race selective.

Robert required a meeting so he could let us know the ground rules and we could finalize the agreement. Melanie looked at the calendar, came up with March 23rd and reserved airline tickets. Meanwhile, I continued my efforts to find a reliable travel agent who knew how to make all the connections in Argentina. You would think this was a simple task—we do live in Washington DC, the nation's capitol. You'd be wrong.

Eric C Anderson

The first travel agent I spoke with outright declared it would be impossible to cover that much ground in a 10-day time period. The second said she would get back to me. Never did. The third came up with an estimated cost that made a safari look reasonable. And the fourth sent me a bunch of pictures and then promptly dropped out of sight. Keep all this in mind the next time someone tells you America is transitioning to a service economy. Let's stick with manufacturing, service appears a leap we are not prepared to make now or in the foreseeable future.

Melanie, as she is wont to do, rapidly grew weary of my whining about the "travel agent blues" and went on line to find a suitable replacement. Not surprisingly, she struck gold on the first attempt. An enterprising young man based in California who spent about half the year in Argentina. He not only knew how to get from point A to point B, he had stayed at all the hotels and eaten in many of the restaurants. Oh, and he called back when promised and sent very clear emails. Why can't I find this type of service? Within a week he had an itinerary we could live with and afford. We even had flight reservations that would get us out of the country four days after meeting with Robert.

Now I was psyched. We have the adoption dance back in step with the music, a vacation to Argentina in the bag, and I've passed the poly. Oh, yeah, the poly. Less than a week after my first waltz with the truth doctors I was back on the bike headed for Dulles. Sometimes it can take a month before they can book you for a repeat session in the chair. This time I got lucky. Seems a large number of folks cancelled their session in the happy room and my name came up on the random number generator. Pull on the leathers, fire up the cigar, and put Warren in the bike's CD player. They're ready and I'm ready.

The young lady who served as the interrogator for the second round was spared one onerous duty, no need for the hand warmer…temperatures were a positively balmy 35. The knuckles

Adopting Ainsley

were red, but not frozen. She did, however, have the unfortunate responsibility of determining my veracity. That is, she had to determine if my resume was a complete lie or simply the standard collection of exaggerations. The former is bad, the latter is simply unfortunate. You see, I can be blackmailed for lying—I can only get hired for waxing poetic about my previous employment performance.

Want to know what the poly folks didn't believe? They didn't think I actually have a PhD. Go figure. I think it'd just normal for someone with too much time in academia to travel on a motorcycle and have ink etched into his skin. I'd be wrong. And the poly folks were going to be the first to let me know. Over the course of more than three hours I got to answer a lot of questions concerning my credentials and capabilities. Well, mostly my credentials. At the end of this session the young lady looked at me and asked, "How do you think you did?" I looked her square in the eye and declared, "I passed." Worked for me, appeared to work for her. No session three. Time to start thinking about how much good food and drink we will enjoy in the foothills of Argentina.

Chapter XVII
The Best Laid Plans

To promise not to do a thing is the surest way in the world to make a body want to go and do that very thing.
—*Mark Twain*

I am not so vain as to believe I can control the whimsy of fate. To ward off a sense of gloom that otherwise might be associated with this realist's perspective on life, I indulge in a heady dose of fiction. The fiction that everything will turn out well in the end. (It won't…none of us will get out of here alive.) The fiction 90 percent of my planned activities for any given day will be accomplished. (This is a real bit of fantasy…ever try to finish everything on the to-do list when confronted with at least an hour of commuting, a house built in 1890, and a dog?) And, the fiction we were going to be on vacation in Argentina while attempting to adopt.

Recall my admonition back a dozen chapters or so? No adoption opportunity will arise until one has other plans in hand—usually a long-awaited vacation? Well add to that a scheduled trip to meet with a new adoption attorney. I can't blame Harvey for Mike's piss-poor performance, nor can I blame him for a failure to find potential birthmothers—but I was willing to sacrifice rationality for the good, old-fashioned human tendency to hold others up to a standard we could not meet ourselves. Think of it this way, we all condemn lackluster service when eating out, speaking with an info technology helpdesk, or returning goods the day after Christmas. I know. I've caught myself saying, "I could do this better with my eyes closed." But could you? Well, could you?

If you just answered yes, you're lying. Now please allow me to set aside the soapbox and get back to our story. Rational or not,

Harvey's head was on the chopping block. Melanie was certain Robert could answer the mail, and I was certain Melanie was right. I may not be rational, but I'm not stupid. When Melanie comes up with a plan it's best to go along with the prescribed course of action. She had put a meeting with Robert on the calendar and that was that. I was just hoping he could deliver on a small person before I would be attending that child's high school graduation wearing Depends and using a walker.

Melanie assured me that was indeed the case and then came home with several travel books covering Argentina from head to toe. Back to our standard division of labor. Melanie was searching for restaurants, while I set about determining which sights were must see, vice pure hype. The waterfall was a must see, the wine country was a must see, Buenos Aires was way high on the list, Patagonia…well, Patagonia was suffering a lack of spousal support. Melanie had done a little digging on the side. Patagonia promised glaciers, windswept vistas, and a bit of cowboy ruggedness. It did not, however, offer a surplus of good eating, warm weather, or hotels featuring 400 thread-count sheets.

I did my best to make up for the shortfalls with promises of staying at a working ranch, riding horses, and even hiking along lakes said to be South America's version of the Alps. Yup, not working for me. See, you have been paying attention. By now you know Melanie is not taken with any of these "amusements." Nonetheless, by the second week of March she consented to Patagonia so long as I made up for the "suffering" by agreeing to not walk us to death in Buenos Aires. Done deal, I spit on my hand and went to shake so as to formalize the pact. Melanie just rolled her eyes and mumbled "boys." Hey, it worked in middle school.

Meantime, fate was creeping up on our best laid plans. In late February, a young woman from Ohio contacted an adoption attorney in Los Angeles. Takimia, was 23, single mother of a 3 year-old boy, and working on her associate's degree. She had made the unfortunate mistake of going out for a night's partying and landed up pregnant. Yeah, yeah. I see the moralistic headshaking. Like none of you have ever had unprotected sex before. Anyway, five months later she realized a decision had to be made. Abortion was out, and she could not afford to raise another child. This left two options, tell her family and rely on kin, or contact an adoption attorney.

So here's where the quiz kicks in. Remember the boring adoption statistics I rattled off much earlier in our story? What? No instant recall...I should hold my breath and go on an author's harrumph to the other side of the room. Never mind. Here's the numbers. About 1.7% of children born to never-married white women are placed for adoption. That figure drops to between 0.2 and 1.5% for never-married black women. Takimia is African-American. If you asked me, our odds of speaking with her were somewhere safely between zero and nothing. One look at me, and the figure was likely to be "absolutely impossible."

After considerable soul-searching, Takimia ruled out option one. She decided the best hope for her son was to get an education, and that was not going to happen with another small child in the house. This meant, however, she could not tell her extended family about the decision to go with adoption. Put yourself in her shoes, not a decision I would want to struggle through. Not only will the family be peeved when they find out, they will likely hold this over your head forever. Friends will forgive you, family, not likely. An angry family member is always happy to pull out the nuclear club and use it on the guilty. This was indeed a nuclear club.

Here's where courage comes into the picture. You and I may have no spine. Takimia was not so handicapped. She made the hard choice and contacted a one David Ellis, private adoption attorney at large. This really had to be a case of the odd couple. Takimia was calling from blue collar Ohio, David is the most L.A. guy you will ever meet. When I turn 60 I want to fit in David's shoes.

Eric C Anderson

Tanned, fit, and cool to the core. He plays beach tennis, drives a BMW, and works his own hours. His wife handles the finances, and he worries about enjoying the weather. David is a vintage Californian. That is to say, what a Californian was before Arnold Schwarzenegger got hold of the state.

David has been in the adoption business a long, long time. So long, in fact, he sold one practice, retired, and then went back to work in the same field as a hobby. This experience and his evident success came from hard work and adherence to some very simple rules. Rule one: Make sure the birthmother really was committed to the idea of adoption. Rule two: About four weeks before the baby was due, fly mom to L.A. Why? This prevents friends and family from trying to talk her out of adoption—and it sets the stage for a relatively straightforward legal transaction once the baby is born. As I noted previously, California is an adoption-friendly state.

David was sticking with his rules in dealing with Takimia. Scheduled to deliver her child sometime during the second week of April, he flew her to L.A. in mid-March. He then began to process of introducing Takimia to potential adoptive parents. This is where my wonderful cut and paste brochure—the one extolling our virtues—comes back into the picture. Takimia was provided a handful of these slick publications and asked to think about possible options for her daughter. The first pile went back to David… no dice.

David pulled out a second pile and provided that stack to Takimia. She went back her hotel room and poured over the letters and pictures. Tough work if you think about it.

Here you are, a pregnant woman, about to deliver, and you are being asked to decide on the child's fate by reading single page letters or glancing at cute parent pictures. I make decisions about auto and motorcycle purchases in such a manner, I would not want to go shopping for parents in a similar fashion. But that was all Da-

Adopting Ainsley

vid could offer Takimia—he could not request would-be parents fly to California for a meeting until she had made a choice. I get a headache just thinking about this.

Ok, so here's where I get to pick on my friends in the medical career field. Mothers have been delivering babies since...since Adam and Eve....or some such. In other words, a long time. And we all know the standard gestation period for a human is somewhere around nine months. Underline somewhere. Why? Because doctors are unable to accurately predict when a particular human being is going to exit the womb. "Too many variables," is the standard excuse. I think it's just plain intellectual laziness, but I'm just a political scientist who likes to pound on computer keyboards—not determining birthdates by watching blood pressure and listening to heart beats.

Anyway, both David and Takimia had listened to the doctors and were convinced she was not going into labor for another three weeks, plenty of time to go through the parent brochures and sort the wheat from the chafe. Their best laid plans were also about to go out the door. On the 22nd of March, Takimia went into labor. And we're not talking simple breathing pain or indigestion. We're talking full on...this baby is coming out...labor. At that point she called David and made two points absolutely clear. One, she needed to be brought to a hospital. Two, she needed a final stack of potential prospects.

David met both requests. But before he headed for Takimia's hotel, David made one more cycle through his list of business contacts. There, near the bottom of his rollodesk, was Harvey Schweitzer, the Maryland-based attorney who David spoke with on an irregular basis. The phone call was made. Harvey confirmed that, yes, he did have clients who wanted to adopt a child on short notice and were very open to all races. Harvey then faxed—faxed—David a copy of our carefully constructed brochure. So much for the pink construction paper, hand-pasted photos, and fancy ribbon binding. Takimia's first exposure to Melanie and I was via a smeared, barely legible, black and white fax of our bid to become parents. A fax. Damn good thing Melanie knows how to write a compelling letter. According to Takimia, she could not even see our pictures on the fax paper.

Meanwhile, we're sitting at home preparing to fly to Florida for a meeting with Robert. The overnight bag is packed, my computer is jammed into a briefcase, and Melanie is surfing for a television show that will take the edge off another day of dealing with official Washington. Harvey had informed Melanie a baby was about to be born in California and that he had forwarded our information to the attorney working in L.A…and then the phone had gone cold. Given our previous experiences there was no way we were going to become optimistic or even overly interested in this situation.

That *laissez-faire* attitude vanished at about 7:30pm. There we were sitting on the couch, dabbling at ice cream, when a paralegal in David's office called to say a prospective birthmother had just delivered a healthy baby girl. Melanie confirmed that we were interested in learning more about a potential placement and almost went back to the ice cream. I told you we were calloused adoption professionals by this point. Even a call about a child standing by for immediate acquisition was not cause for jubilation. Well, maybe not completely calloused. Melanie hung up and called David.

David carefully explained that Takimia had selected us from a stack of other families and wanted to discuss the option of our becoming parents to her daughter. Now Melanie and I were paying attention—a lot of attention. The ice cream went in the sink. They'll make more ice cream, we knew opportunities like this were not so predictable. Takimia asked a lot of questions (kicking the tires, if you will). She wanted to know about our backgrounds, why we wanted to adopt, and how we felt about adopting an African American child. She also wanted to know how we would raise a child…a lot of reading was important, as was an emphasis on education.

We must have answered appropriately. Takimia said she wanted to meet us and requested that we fly out to California for a face-to-face. Melanie and I looked at each other, hugged, and then began dashing about the house. With military precision, Melanie managed to get us on the "beautiful people express (the previously mentioned direct flight from Reagan-National Airport to L.A.), I grabbed another suitcase and jammed in some light reading. Hey, if we were going to be spending time in a hotel, I wanted it to be productive time. I told you I believe in fiction. Ever spend nights in a hotel room with a child who is two days old? Sorry, I'm getting ahead of myself.

A night of fitful sleeping later, we showed up at the airport 60 minutes ahead of schedule. Melanie was taking no chances on missing the flight. But more importantly, she was waiting for a phone call from David offering assurance that Takimia had not changed her mind in the last 12 hours. Here's the trick, we still had not cancelled the meeting with Robert. So we're standing at the check-in counter with tickets to L.A. and to Florida. If Takimia backed out—a very real possibility—we were going to find a new manager for the team. Unlike George Steinbrenner, we were not giving Harvey the five chances offered Billy Martin. One losing season was enough.

Thirty minutes before our scheduled take off David called. Takimia was insistent we were the ones. Before I could even offer a high-five, Melanie was on the line with Robert's office. "Many thanks for your willingness to take us on as clients, but we think we have a firm adoption happening as we speak." Robert graciously offered a congratulations and then kindly declared he would be willing to help should the need arise. Wow, this guy really was a class act. What was he doing in the adoption business? Seems to me he would have been better off representing wayward bankers or wealthy white collar criminals.

This closed the loose ends. We flew to L.A. in style. Rather than sit in coach with the other strap hangers, we upgraded to first class. Melanie and I figured there would be plenty of time for poverty over the next 25 years. Oh, did I mention Melanie insist I dress like an adult and leave the plastic bags at home? She was taking no chances on this opportunity. My normal travel attire and preference for a disposable briefcase were not an option. Guess what, gussied up in a pair of kakis and a nice button-down shirt, even I can look presentable.

Good thing Melanie insisted on adult attire. We landed in L.A. and ran for the rental car lots. Just as with my attire, Melanie was taking no chances with L.A. traffic. Adding more stress to the moment, we were headed directly for the hospital. David had directed we meet with Takimia as soon as possible. This was all coming together at a speed I would never have predicted. But first we had to get to the hospital—this required Melanie take on the role of navigating the maze that is southern California. And not running down the "idiots" who were stalling our sense of destiny.

Valley Presbyterian, the hospital in question, is a tough place. Or at least it has a tough clientele. How tough? Even the toilet seats in the public bathrooms were covered in graffiti. (A psychologist would have a great time taking apart the sense of self-worth someone must have when etching their name on a toilet lid, but that's a subject for another day…we're in the midst of an adoption here.) Sitting up in a bed on the fourth floor was the young lady who would change our lives forever. Takimia looked tired and a bit apprehensive. Lying next to her was the smallest child I had ever seen—a child who joined this world weighing 5lbs 8ozs and measuring all of about 18 inches. Tiny.

Adopting Ainsley

Try striking up a conversation in this setting. Not a whole lot of small talk to be made. We asked about how Takimia was doing. "Fine." Ok, that's not working. We asked if she had questions for us. "Why do you want to adopt?" Melanie gave the five minute version of this story and then stressed our focus on education and family. So far so good. I heard no disapproving tone or context in the conversation. "Are you ready to be parents?" There's a good question. We lied. "Absolutely." Same answer parents around the world provide. We are all wrong.

"I'd like you to be parents for my daughter." Finally, the words we had waited so long to hear. There were hugs, Melanie wiped a few tears from her eyes, and it was over. At least the informal part. The great paperwork chase was yet to be finished.

Epilogue

Conformity—the natural instinct to passively yield to that vague something recognized as authority.

—*Mark Twain*

If we could have flown home that night, Melanie would have already booked the flight. Things are never that simple, particularly when dealing with adoption. We left the hospital and I took the car keys. Melanie was already furiously at work on the phone. She tracked down Harvey to ensure the homestudy was headed to the appropriate bureaucrats. She hunted down David to ensure he was lining up the stack of documents we needed to sign. And she set up a dinner reservation at one of her favorite places in downtown L.A. All that happened before I was even able to get out of the hospital parking lot. One of these days I am going to have to contemplate acquiring one of those Blackberry things—my old cell phone does nothing that efficiently.

The discussion with David proved the most nerve-wracking of the three conversations. Harvey was happy to have our business; the restaurant apparently felt similarly, David proved less reassuring. Before we could take Ainsley…we we already referring to her by that name…out of the hospital Takimia had to sign away her parental rights and we had to get a social worker to do a final hand wave over our suitability to serve as parents.

California provides two options for potential birthmothers when it comes to signing away their rights. They can choose to wait 30 days. Or, they can sign immediately and the decision goes into effect within 72 hours. Takimia had declared a willingness to use the latter option, but this complicated the proceedings. In order to prevent potential arm-twisting via the attorney handling the adoption, she would have to see yet another lawyer. This meant more legal bills for us, but far less angst in the long run. We immediately agreed to cover the expense.

The social worker option was less convenient. According to David, he had a specific individual lined up to handle this case. She was said to be quick, efficient, and by the book. All the things Melanie required from anyone working in government. The drawback, she maintained an office 30 miles south of L.A. We were incredulous. There was no one closer than 30 miles south of the nation's worst commuting nightmare. David came back with a firm "No" and then provided directions. Seems we were driving south.

So far so good. The restaurant proved an excellent choice. I don't know why I expected otherwise. Melanie is always on her game in that department. The hotel served the purpose. Air conditioning worked, bed was not too lumpy and the kitchenette was clean. We slept poorly for a second night, but what do you expect? Melanie was worrying the last minute issues and I was worrying this whole second running at fatherhood.

The morning came early. I sprinted for the gym after finding a *New York Times* for Melanie and then we headed off to breakfast with David and his wife. A small mountain of paperwork waited at our table. Disclosures, nondisclosures, amendments, nonamendments, agreements, nonagreements. I don't know what it all meant, as best I could tell it was a whole stack of legal stuff that my attorney, the one I'm married to, said I should simply sign. So I did. This was no time for my usual questions about the fine print.

Then it was back into the car and a dash for some office complex in the far suburbs. We arrived at 8:45. The receptionist looked at us funny and offered a very uncomfortable couch. "The doctor," we were formally instructed, "does not arrive before nine." Great, 15 minutes of sitting on a couch while Melanie repeatedly glanced

Adopting Ainsley

at her Blackberry and worried return traffic. I read the *Times*. We waited—like Jake and Elliot in the "Blues Brothers" closing scene.

At 9 o'clock the lady in question breezed through the door, made no attempt to glance our direction, and headed straight for her office. I thought Melanie was going to spring off the couch like a bull terrier ready to worry a rat to death. Instead she calmly walked up to the haughty receptionist and asked to please inform the "doctor" we were waiting. The lady behind the counter nodded her head and went back to surfing the web. Melanie came and sat back down. Hmmm, interesting behavior, not exactly what I expected.

At 09:15, the "doctor" reappeared and beckoned us into her office. This was a work to behold. Bedecked with dusty psychology texts and a couple of over-stuffed couches, this place had not seen the sun...or a cleaning crew...in years. It did; however, appear to be a site favored by aging hippies. The art work was right out of 1968, and the background music had to be the Grateful Dead. We really were in southern California. The matron who resided behind the sealed venetian blinds bid us to have a seat and then asked a sequence of vanilla questions about our desire to adopt. At that point she signed three official documents and wished us good luck. All very strange, not sure I understand what happened to this day.

We walked out to the car and began the race back to the hospital. As far as we knew, all that was left was to pick up our daughter...the car seat was already installed. The final moments of this whole charade were pulling into view...almost.

By the time we climbed back to the fourth floor—the elevators were out of service—perhaps to remove some of the graffiti and thereby allow for actual reading of the buttons, Takimia had been released. The nursing staff politely informed us that the baby could be found in the nursery and then escorted Melanie and

Eric C Anderson

me through a maze of hallways and security doors. I'm bringing breadcrumbs the next time I go to a hospital; these places have all proven beyond my capacity to recall left from right. In any case, we found the nursery, a warm alcove with rocking chairs and the usual collection of loving staff. Again, where do they find these people?

There, in her own plastic crib, was our Ainsley, peacefully asleep and—according to the staff—quite comfortable with her place in the world. None of the piercing screeches emitting from some of the other like accommodations. I was handed our daughter and a bottle. Melanie was assigned the task of winning our release. You see, the staff was more than a little suspicious about the claim Ainsley was indeed our daughter. Melanie certainly did not look like a mother who had just given birth and Ainsley, well Ainsley was clearly not our biological daughter. Paperwork, lots of paperwork. Again, damn good thing to have one's own lawyer on hand 24-hours a day.

It took us three hours to escape the hospital. Between security and the billing department…nothing, absolutely nothing in life is free…we signed another mountain of documents. The young lady who was about to become our very own small person slept through the entire affair. So when people ask, how did you finally bring home this darling child? I offer a glass of scotch on the rocks, light a cigar, and begin laying out the tale of adopting Ainsley.

Eric C. Anderson
1 August 2011

About the Author

Eric C. Anderson is faculty member at the National Intelligence University. As a long-standing member of the U.S. intelligence community, he has written over 600 articles for the National Intelligence Council, International Security Advisory Board and the Department of Defense. In addition, he is a leading scholar on the rise of sovereign wealth funds. His book, *Take the Money and Run: Sovereign Wealth Funds and the Demise of American Prosperity* was published in March 2009. A long-time student of all things Northeast Asia, Mr Anderson published *China Restored: The Middle Kingdom Looks to 2020 and Beyond* in 2010.

Prior to assuming his current position, Mr. Anderson served as a national security consultant and a senior intelligence analyst. He has worked for the Defense Intelligence Agency, the Multi National Forces-Iraq in Baghdad and at the U.S. Pacific Command in Hawaii. From 1990-2000, Mr. Anderson was an active duty intelligence officer in the United States Air Force—with assignments in Japan, Korea and Saudi Arabia. He remains on duty as an Air Force reserve officer. He has also taught for the University of Missouri, University of Maryland, and the Air Force Academy.

Mr. Anderson has a PhD in political science from the University of Missouri, a MA from Bowling Green State University in Ohio, and a BA from Illinois Wesleyan University. He is a graduate of the Air Force Squadron Officer's School, Air Command and Staff College, and the Air War College. A long-time Harley rider, Mr. Anderson claims to have put over 200,000 miles on motorcycles during the last 20 years…and looks forward to his daughter joining him on the highways and byways that call every wind-blown gypsy.

Endnotes

1. Bradford Winslow, Kenton Voorhees, and Katherine Pehl, 15 October 2007, "Methamphetamine Abuse," American Family Physician, Volume 76, Number 8, pp. 1169-1174.
2. Susan Okie, 27 January 2009, "The Epidemic that Wasn't," *New York Times*, p. D1.

www.ingramcontent.com/pod-product-compliance
Lightning Source LLC
LaVergne TN
LVHW051829080426
835512LV00018B/2794